PARTNERS IN INTIMACY

Living Christian Marriage Today

Challon O'Hearn Roberts
William P. Roberts

PAULIST PRESS • NEW YORK / MAHWAH

Book design by Ellen Whitney

Copyright © 1988 by
William P. Roberts and Challon O'Hearn Roberts

All rights reserved. No part of this book may be reproduced or transmitted in any form or by any means, electronic or mechanical, including photocopying, recording or by any information storage and retrieval system without permission in writing from the Publisher.

Library of Congress Cataloging-in-Publication Data

Roberts, Challon O'Hearn, 1940-
    Partners in intimacy: living Christian marriage today / Challon O' Hearn Roberts, William P. Roberts.
    p. cm.
    ISBN 0-8091-3006-8 (pbk.):
    1. Marriage—Religious aspects—Catholic Church. 2. Catholic Church—Doctrines. I. Roberts, William P. II. Title.
BX2250.R63 1988
248.8'4—dc19   88-15229
                                                                                 CIP

Published by Paulist Press
997 Macarthur Boulevard
Mahwah, NJ 07430

Printed and bound in the
United States of America

Table of Contents

Introduction.. 1
Chapter 1 Marriage as Partnership.................. 3
Chapter 2 Marital Intimacy 17
Chapter 3 Two for Dialogue........................ 30
Chapter 4 Sexual Intimacy 55
Chapter 5 Co-Parenting............................ 76
Chapter 6 The Place of Work....................... 97
Chapter 7 Money Matters 108
Chapter 8 Old and New Relationships..............123
Chapter 9 Marriage with a Difference 137
Chapter 10 Marriage and Christian Discipleship....153

Introduction

The term "marriage" will most probably conjure up as many meanings as there are marriages. Marriages can range all the way from bitter, hostile battlegrounds to havens of peace and love; from convenient arrangements to unions of profound, personal commitment; from distant co-existence to intimate closeness and sharing. What spells the difference between these dramatically disparate models? Why can that trip to the altar result in such diverse consequences? What can a couple do to control the destiny of their marriage and direct it toward a growing intimacy? These are the kinds of questions that are the concern of this book.

An earlier work[1] examined the meaning of marriage in light of Christian faith. Marriage between two Christians is meant to be a sacrament, a dynamic sign of Christ's love. By living out their commitment to Christ in their marriage, a couple allows God's truth and love, God's peace, justice and holiness to influence the way they relate to each other, their children and the wider community. In this way the couple engage in true Christian service. They also become a sign of Christ's self-giving: this is my body given for you.

We wish in this present book to deal with practical ways of achieving the kind of marital intimacy implied in that theology. After we explore the meaning of marital intimacy, we take up the major elements of marriage and address some of the key issues that face a married couple in today's world.

This book is addressed primarily to married couples and to those preparing for marriage. It does not have as its purpose the offering of definitive answers and final solutions to the complexities of marriage. What we write is meant to stimulate thought, discussion and analysis. Hopefully, the reader will integrate what is deemed helpful, and disregard what seems inapplicable. To aid in this process, questions and suggestions for reflection and discussion are appended to each chapter. Each series of discussion exercises is divided into three sections: for all readers, for married couples, for engaged couples. It might be helpful in the exercises for couples for each person to write her/his answers first, and then the couple can dialogue about what they have written.

In all of the examples in this book names have been changed, and sometimes circumstances altered, to protect confidentiality. We wish to express our thanks to Robert Hamma, editor at Paulist Press, for his guidance and support throughout the writing of this book. We are also grateful to Mary Lynn Naughton for typing the manuscript.

Notes

[1] William P. Roberts, *Marriage: Sacrament of Hope and Challenge* (Cincinnati: St. Anthony Messenger Press, 1983).

Chapter 1

Marriage as Partnership

Is marriage dead, or is it going through birth pains? Is it crumbling toward disintegration, or is it moving toward new and richer forms? Has marriage seen its day, or are the brightest times just over the horizon?

The voice of the cynic, heard in many corners today, proclaims the death of marriage and the end of days never again to be matched for their marital bliss. The conviction of this book, on the other hand, is that a new day in the history of marriage has begun to dawn. Yes, the human race is going through troubled decades as far as marriage is concerned. But the trauma which marriage as an institution is experiencing is not that of the death rattle, but of a rebirth. The present troubles are rooted, to a great extent, in new understandings of marriage, gender, and sexuality, and in the search for more meaningful forms in which these insights can be translated. Few people are satisfied with marriages that are kept together either "for the sake of the children" or out of economic necessity. Past models of marriage that were built on notions of male supremacy and the subservience of wives to their husbands no longer fit in an age of feminist consciousness-raising. Sex within marriage is no longer identified primarily with procreation, but is appreciated for the benefits it brings to a couple and to their relationship, as well as to their children.

In the past few decades there has been a dramatic shift toward a more personalist approach to marriage. This shift is reflected in the radical change that has taken place in official Catholic teaching regarding marriage. For centuries the Church had spoken of marriage as a contract in which the couple give each other the right over their bodies for acts of sexual intercourse that are of themselves suitable for procreation. In this understanding, the first purpose of marriage was procreation; relational aspects were secondary.[1]

The bishops at the Second Vatican Council, on the other hand, departed from the legal language of the past. They spoke, instead, of marriage as a covenant and as an "intimate partnership of married life and love." In marriage spouses mutually exchange the gift of themselves in love. They "render mutual help and service to each other through an intimate union of their persons and of their actions."[2]

This shift toward a more personalist understanding of marriage is an important, hopeful sign. It reflects the fact that a growing number of couples are searching and working for more profound and richer relationships with their spouses. While a personalist understanding of marriage places more challenges and demands on married couples, it also presents an ideal for more mutually satisfying marriages and hence will insure the future of marriage as a strong and healthy institution.

In this chapter we shall reflect on this personalist dimension of marriage. What does it mean to say that marriage is a partnership of life and love? What are some practical ways in which couples can grow in this life of partnership?

The Qualities of Partnership

Marital partnership implies mutual choice and equality of persons. Unlike partnerships that are limited by professional or business interests, the partnership of marriage embraces all of life and love. Each of these elements, basic to marital partnership, needs to be explored.

Mutual Choice. Mutual choice means that the couple freely select each other as marriage partners. They form their unique partnership by freely giving of themselves to one another and receiving each other. This mutual gift, formally bestowed and accepted at the wedding ceremony, is repeated countless times daily as the couple grow in their union. All of the interactions, great and small, that comprise the routine of married life can become a sign of the couple's ongoing desire to grow as mutual gift for one another.

In contemporary Western culture this choice of a partner is based on earlier free choices in the dating situation. We choose whom we date. We decide whether to get serious in a relationship. We select the person with whom we become engaged. This is in contrast with those cultures where the selection of a mate is arranged by the parents, and the couple ratify that selection by their consent at the wedding ceremony.

This means that we become responsible not only for the promises we make at the altar, but also for all of the decisions that have led up to that moment. The mutual choice on the wedding day, then, is the culmination of a long series of earlier choices. It is also the beginning of a lifetime of confirming choices that will take place on a daily basis throughout the marriage, as well as in the moments of crisis that are inevitable in every marital union.

Equality of Persons. If taken seriously, "partnership," as applied to marriage, must ring the death knell for male chauvinist views of marriage. If wife and husband are true partners, then they are on an equal standing as far as the marriage is concerned. A view that sees the wife as inferior to her husband, based on the notion that women are, after all, inferior to men, does violence to the notion of partnership. An approach to marriage that demands the wife be subordinate to her husband does not regard the female spouse as a true partner. Any expectation that the wife must "obey" her husband, without any necessity on his part to "obey" his wife, is at odds with the essential notion of partnership.[3]

For marriage to be a true partnership, wife and husband must regard each other as human beings who are equal in dignity. They must acknowledge the fact that both have equal human rights, and are equally deserving of regard and consideration. They need to respect the rights each has to privacy, to develop their unique talents and gifts, and to make certain personal decisions.

To say that wife and husband are partners in the marriage is to say that together they are co-heads, co-founders, co-authors of the marital community that we call family. If they are partners, he is *not* the head of the house. *They* both are.

Partnership of Life. In marriage spouses share their lives with one another. They commit themselves for life. The words "for life" have a double meaning. Spouses commit themselves to each other for the duration of their life. They also pledge themselves to be for the life of one another and to enrich each other's lives. This sharing and enrichment involves all the dimensions of human life: the physical, intellectual, emotional and spiritual.

On the physical level married people share their residence, their bed and their board. They concern themselves with the bodily health and well-being of one another, and address each other's physical needs. This level of sharing is understood as basic to every marriage.

Marriage between two human persons demands that we share what distinguishes us from the rest of the animal kingdom: our minds. An integral part of our partnership is to "put our heads together," share our thoughts and insights, our diverse opinions and points of view, and create new vistas.

For many couples it is much more difficult to share on the emotional level than on the physical and intellectual levels. It takes insight, intuition and sensitivity for a couple to understand, accept and respond to their own emotional needs and the needs of their partner.

Even spouses who are very generous in addressing a spouse's physical demands can be blind to some of the deeper emotional needs. How many spouses, well taken care of on the physical level, are left emotionally starving? How often in the counseling room have we heard a spouse say: "I don't know why s/he walked out on me? I provided a nice home, plenty of food, two cars?" The other side of the story reveals that the mate felt that her/his emotional needs were never addressed in any adequate fashion. While the sharing of the physical dimension of our lives is fundamental, the quality of marriage is directly related to how well we are able to share our lives on the emotional level.

Finally, our lives have a religious or "spiritual" dimension. In one way or another each of us is confronted by God. We are faced with timeless questions: "Is there anything to life beyond what meets the eye?" "What, if anything, awaits us beyond the grave?" "Is it worth being honest and decent and just?" "Is there Someone who ultimately cares?" Somewhere in the depth of our being, every one of us must grapple with these questions and shape our lives according to the answers we choose to embrace.

In marriage we commit ourselves to share this deeper, most personal, and perhaps less "certain" dimension of our lives with each other. We become partners in our journey of faith. We allow the Spirit of God within us to touch each other through our giving and our receiving.

Partnership of Love. In the not too distant past, while we claimed that marriage was a loving relationship, we often spoke of it in terms of authority and obedience. And, of course, the role of authority figure, of "head of the house," was given to the husband, while the obligation of obedience was imposed on the wife.

Even if, enlightened by the feminist movement, we shift from those stereotypes to a model of mutual obedience, we are left with a very inadequate model for marriage. Marriage is a partnership of love, not a partnership of obedience. The ultimate virtue in the Bible is not obedience but love. In any authority-obedience encounter, regardless of how benevolent it be, there is ultimately a "ruler" and one who is "ruled," a "superior" and a "subordinate." In any conflict which is settled by one person having the "final say" and imposing her/his will on the other, there is a "winner" and a "loser."

In our opinion, there is no room for this kind of a model in marriage. In marriage we do not pledge ourselves to obey each other. We make a solemn commitment to love each other. Marriage is not about taking and receiving orders. It is about intuiting the feelings, needs, and desires of the other and sensitively responding to these. In marriage we solve conflicts by sharing and listening to each other's points of view and agreeing to come to some consensus with which we can both be comfortable.

However, having said that marriage is a partnership of love and not of obedience, we are left with the nagging question "What is love?" Of all the various "definitions" of love we have come across, we find the one offered by M. Scott Peck in *The Road Less Travelled* more practical than most. Love, Peck states, is "the will to extend one's self for the purpose of nurturing one's own or another's spiritual growth" (p. 81). Let us share some of our own reflections on this definition.

Love is an act of the will. It is a choice. It is not just a feeling or a desire to love the other. We freely choose to love the other and to enact that choice by the only way in which authentic love is shown, namely by *acting* in a genuinely loving way.

Love involves extending ourselves. We go beyond ourselves and our mere self-interest. We reach out to another. We take the interest of another to heart. We put ourselves out for the sake of the other.

The last part of Peck's definition specifies the significance of the motive or purpose for extending oneself. Not every extension of oneself "on behalf of another" is genuine love. Some people have dominated others in the name of "love," and in the process have crushed their spirit. It is possible to "smother" another with love and thus prevent the person from becoming who s/he is meant to be.

Authentic love is shown by actions that nurture one's own and another's spiritual growth. First, this means that there is a link between love of self and love of another. Any authentic expression of love of oneself will enable one to love and enrich others more. Any authentic expression of love for another makes one a more loving and, hence, a better person.

Second, love nourishes our *spiritual* growth. Here, however, we interpret the word "spiritual" as it was used in the Hebrew Bible: *not* "spirit" in opposition to "body," but "embodied spirit," "inspirited body." To grow spiritually means to grow in a full way. Hence, true love is an extension of oneself in order to promote the total well-being both of oneself and the other. True love nurtures growth on the physical, intellectual, emotional and spiritual levels and contributes to the integration of these dimensions in a person. Love, in other words, is holistic and furthers the process of holism in oneself and in others.

To say, then, that marriage is a partnership of love is to claim that in marriage both spouses give and extend themselves to each other in ways that nourish their total growth. They spend their lives learning how to love and striving to accomplish this love. The only true test of the quality of their love is the life-giving and growth-giving effect they have on each other.

Practical Applications

Having reflected on the personalist approach that views marriage as a partnership of life and love, let us turn to some practical ways that can lead to a mutually fulfilling union.

Mutual Choice. Two things can particularly help promote an environment of freedom with which couples can choose each other in marriage. First, parents, and society at large can remove any pressure on people to get married.

The expectation that all "normal" persons get married in their twenties, disparaging comments regarding persons who are single, and suspicions about "what is wrong" with one's daughter or son who is not yet seriously dating can all exercise subtle forms of pressure.

Second, it is quite beneficial that before two people get very serious about each other, and get locked into an exclusive relationship, they date other people. This can provide a more balanced perspective in regard to one's chosen mate.

It is also important that in the dating relationship the couple respect each other's freedom in regard to the pace of the growing relationship. One ought not to pressure the other into exclusive dating, or into a serious commitment, or into an earlier wedding date until both are ready and equally comfortable in taking together whatever the next step is. When one partner is ready to get more serious sooner than the other is, they need to talk frankly about how they feel and take measures to adjust the relationship in ways that are reasonably suitable to both.

Self-Gift. In order for a person to make a gift of oneself to another, one must look upon oneself as a good person, as one who is gifted, as one who is worth enough to be a gift. If I cannot see myself as gift, how can I give of myself in gift to another?

Giving a gift is always risky business. Giving the gift of self is even more risky. Every gift can be rejected. In order to take the risk of having the gift of myself rejected, I must accept myself. Then, despite any rejections, one's sense of self-dignity is left intact.

One of the very important preparations for giving oneself in marriage, then, is the building of self-esteem. This is a process that begins at the earliest stages of life and must be nurtured into adulthood. Among the many ways in which we can build our self-esteem, the following are especially worthy of note:

(1) Concentrate on your good points: your talents, gifts and virtues.

(2) See yourself through the eyes of those who love and cherish you; discover your lovableness through the lovableness that others see in you.

(3) Do not believe the image of yourself derived from those who hate or dislike you; remember that hatred obscures vision; it is love that brings true light.

(4) See your limitations and faults, but see them in the light of your goodness.

(5) Appreciate your uniqueness; there can never be another you; the world is a better place because you are here.

(6) Learn to trust your judgment, and your ability to make good decisions; the mistakes we have made can help us learn for the future.

Finally, marriage also involves receiving and accepting the other as gift. To do so, we need to recognize the giftedness of our mate and to appreciate the gift s/he makes of her/himself. To receive another's gift we have to be able to acknowledge our own incompleteness and our need of how the other complements us and can help us toward wholeness.

Equality of Partners. One of the principal issues that a couple must face before marriage is how they view the relationship between female and male. We list here some representative questions that can help a couple get in touch with where they are regarding this issue.

Do you view the wife-husband relationship in terms of obedience and authority? If so, who must "obey" whom, and under what circumstances? When there is a difference of opinion on an issue, who will make the final decision?

Do you think the husband is head of the house? Why or why not?

On the wedding day, who will take whose family name? What is the significance of how this issue is resolved?

Who will sit at the "head" of your family table? Why?

Who will be expected to make sacrifices for the other's career? Is the wife the one who will be expected to subordinate her career to the husband's?

Do you perceive that the various chores in marriage (e.g., cooking, washing dishes, doing the laundry, cleaning the house, changing diapers, caring for the baby at midnight, cutting the grass, taking out the garbage, and managing the financial books) are already and forever "assigned by God" according to gender stereotypes? Or do you believe that a fair distribution of these tasks at any given period of the marriage ought to be made as a result of dialogue and based on mutual consideration, generosity, and a sense of service to one another?

What is your basic attitude toward sex? Is sex for you divorced from commitment and love? Is sex primarily a male privilege?

These last three questions are particularly pertinent in a culture where many see sex primarily in terms of personal recreation and self-titillation, even at the expense of one's partner, and where we have operated under a double sexual standard that favors the male.

Besides the questions listed above, we believe that it is imperative for every male to do some serious soul-searching in regard to his attitude toward women. Are women perceived as equal in personal dignity to men? Are women looked upon primarily as sex objects or as partners for life and love? Are women respected as intelligent, creative beings who have a God-given call and destiny of their own? Is the fact accepted that a woman has an identity of her own, and does not receive her identity merely in terms of her relationship with a male?

Such soul-searching is of paramount importance in a patriarchal society such as our own, where women have so often been identified in terms of their relationship with men. Such questioning is also relevant because we live in a culture that supports a multi-billion dollar prostitution and pornography business and engages in widespread advertising, all of which reduce women to sex objects and financial commodities. How has this cultural climate affected consciously and unconsciously the way men regard women, and the way women look on themselves?

Summary

In the past several decades there has been a significant shift toward a personalist understanding of marriage. The marital union can be described as a partnership of life and love. It is a commitment on the part of wife and husband to extend themselves for the purpose of each other's growth on every level—physical, intellectual, emotional, and spiritual. To live such a partnership requires ongoing mutual choice to give continually of ourselves to each other and to respect with equity the dignity that each of us has as human persons.

Such a marriage will enable the couple to achieve true intimacy. It is to the topic of intimacy that we now turn.

Reflection Exercises

For All Readers

This chapter speaks of the more recent personalist understanding of marriage. How has this understanding affected people's expectations of marriage?

What are some of the things that spouses must do in a marriage today in order to meet those expectations?

It is said that this personalist understanding of marriage has contributed both to the increase of happier marriages and to the increase of the divorce rate. Do you think that both parts of that statement are true? Why or why not?

For Married Couples

In what ways do you consider your marriage a true partnership of life and love?

What are some specific ways in which each of you could make your marriage an even better partnership?

Are you satisfied that you and your partner treat each other as equal in human dignity?

Are there ways in which patriarchal and sexist views of marriage still manifest themselves in your relationship? If so, what are they?

How can you work together to remove any remnants of patriarchalism and sexism in your marriage?

For Engaged Couples

How free do you feel in terms of the choice you have made and will make of your partner?

Do you feel any pressures to move at a faster pace in your

growing relationship than with what you feel comfortable?

If so, what are these pressures and from where are they coming (e.g., your family, your partner, yourself)?

Reflect on your love for each other in light of Peck's definition quoted in this chapter: love is the "will to extend one's self for the purpose of nurturing one's own or another's spiritual growth." In what ways have you achieved this kind of love in your relationship so far?

Are there elements in your relationship which manifest a lack of this kind of love?

If so, what are they, and how will you address them?

Reflect on the questions regarding equality of partners listed in this chapter.

Notes

[1] 1917 Code of Canon Law, Canons 1012, 1013, 1081.

[2] *Pastoral Constitution on the Church in the Modern World,* #48.

[3] Since this statement may seem to some to contradict the Pauline passage on marriage in Ephesians, the reader may wish to consult William Roberts' treatment of Ephesians 5:21–33 in *Marriage: Sacrament of Hope and Challenge* (Cincinnati: St. Anthony Messenger Press, 1983).

Chapter 2

Marital Intimacy

If it is impossible to define adequately the words "marriage," "love," and "partnership," it may be even more difficult to define "intimacy" in marriage. First, there is a problem putting into words exactly what is meant by the term "marital intimacy." There is a further difficulty in discerning where a relationship crosses over from non-intimacy into intimacy, and in distinguishing between authentic intimacy and an unhealthy kind of closeness.

Rather than beginning this chapter with an analysis of intimacy, we will look at three kinds of marriages that are at various points on the intimacy spectrum.

George and Rita have been married over thirty years. Their two grown children have left home. They have had no serious marital problems, and only occasional minor disagreements. "We have a good working relationship." George has a full-time job as an accountant. On most evenings and weekends he sells real estate on the side. Rita is a nurse who works the 11 to 7 shift five nights a week. When Rita's mother was widowed eighteen years ago she came to live with them "during the transition period." She is still living with them! Occasionally, however, she does speak of someday getting "her own place." George and Rita have never taken a vacation alone. While they have "an adequate sex life," they spend little time together. George goes on occasional hunting trips with his male friends. Rita and her mother take a weekend away a couple of times a year. "You know how these women are," George proclaims. "The less involved you get with them, the less hassle you will have."

With their twentieth wedding anniversary behind them, Steven and Ellen agree that they have continued to grow closer together with each additional year. They have had a normal number of ups and downs and verbal fights, but they have striven to fight fairly, and have never let the sun go down on their anger. The luncheon phone call, frequent walks, and hours spent chatting on the porch have become an integral part of their relationship. While they each pursue certain hobbies alone and take time to be by themselves, they enjoy being together and sharing each other's interests. Though they put great priority in having regular family dinners with their four teenagers, they make it a point to have occasional late candlelight dinners alone, and to slip out together to a favorite restaurant. Their children enjoy seeing their parents kiss and embrace frequently at home. From time to time Steve likes to surprise Ellen with flowers, and she likes to surprise him with his favorite chocolates.

Bob and Lola, both in their forties, run a small store together. They have no children, and spend virtually all of their workday as well as their leisure time together. They have few friends and do very little socializing. "We have each other, and that's enough for us." Lola goes to all Bob's sports events and watches all his TV programs. Bob joins his wife for her operas, ballets and TV dramas. Bob gets very jealous if Lola spends much time talking to someone else alone. He insists on driving her to and from the beauty salon, the health spa, and the library. When she visits a widow neighbor around the corner he walks her there. When she is about to leave the neighbor's house Lola must call Bob, and he comes to accompany her home.

The above examples obviously describe marriages that are quite different in regard to authentic marital intimacy. George and Rita remain at a distance from each other. Steven and Ellen illustrate a marriage where true intimacy is being achieved. Bob and Lola, on the other hand, manifest a smothering type of closeness.

Let us move from these examples to broader, underlying questions. What are some of the key characteristics of an intimate marriage that distinguishes it from a distant relationship and from an unhealthy kind of closeness? What concrete steps can be taken to create genuine intimacy in one's marriage? We will address these questions by identifying and reflecting on a number of characteristics inherent in an intimate marital relationship.

Mutual Respect. Basic to all intimacy is an attitude of respect that both persons have for each other. While they are each unique and have many differences, they regard each other as persons with the same basic human dignity. They are sensitive to each other's needs and feelings as human beings. They are concerned about the rights each has as humans and they go out of their way to protect those rights. They recognize that their partner deserves to be treated with the same kindness and sensitivity that they expect and desire for themselves.

Where there is mutual respect, there is no place for "putting down" one's partner, or for one person to dominate or "lord it over the other." There is even less place for abusive language, gestures and "jokes" that leave one feeling "inferior." Mutual respect also leads us to avoid the other extreme of patronizing our partner, or of treating our partner in a paternalistic or maternalistic way—the one who patronizes, acts kindly, but in doing so communicates an air of superiority. "Even though you are beneath me, I, in my magnanimity, will be nice to you." To be paternalistic or maternalistic is to treat someone like a child.

Perhaps the image that best captures the mutual respect that spouses ought to have for one another is the one given us in the Bible by the author of the Letter to the Ephesians. We ought to regard each other as we do our own body.

Affection. The external way a couple express their affection for each other depends in part on the personality and upbringing of each. Hence, we want to avoid making a strict correlation between the frequency and kinds of expressions of affection that a couple engage in and the degree of love that exists between them. Nevertheless, having said this, we add our belief that external manifestations of affection have an important place in building intimacy. They are meant to be both a sign of the tender attachment that exists between two people, as well as an important means of nurturing that warmth and closeness.

Our major premise is that manifestations of affection ought not be limited to times of lovemaking, but need to be a regular part of the couple's daily life together. Holding hands, kissing, hugging, and embracing at various times during the course of a day speak loudly of the tender and warm regard that wife and husband have for each other. These expressions of affection also contribute significantly to the ongoing growth of intimate bonding between the couple.

Where children are a part of the marriage, two further benefits accrue from spousal expressions of affection. The warmth that spouses manifest toward each other carries over into the way they express affection toward their children. Secondly, children pick up a great deal about the meaning of marital love and sexuality by observing their parents expressing affection for one another.

Caring. To care for one's spouse is to make her/his well-being a matter of your own foremost priority. It is to be sensitive about how the experiences of life are affecting her/him physically, intellectually, emotionally, and spiritually. Caring means to consider the impact that your words and actions are having on your spouse. It is the willingness to lighten the other's burdens, to ease the struggles of existence, and to make the journey of life a happier, more pleasant experience.

While caring is rooted in the mind and the heart, it is more than an attitude or an emotion. It must be translated into action. To determine the level of their caring, a couple might examine themselves on several points. How do we respond to each other's tears and joys, each other's ups and downs? Do our actions, words, and gestures bring true comfort when the other is troubled? Do they bring affirmation when our partner is besieged with self-doubt? Do they bring support when the other has succeeded? Do we pitch in and help when our spouse is tired? Do we minister when s/he is ill? Do we respond to the unasked request and the non-verbalized desire?

Caring involves the ability to empathize with another person, to feel what s/he feels, to know what it is like to walk in the other's shoes. Caring enables us to put ourselves out for our partner, to be by each other's side and to be for one another a safeguard, a source of support and of nurturing.

Sharing Ideas and Feelings. A couple will grow closer together only to the degree that they are able to share with one another what is unique to human persons, namely, their mind and their heart. There are various levels on which a couple ought to be able to share their thoughts and emotions. On the most superficial level, a couple need to be able to talk about the practicalities of their living together: housing, meals, transportation, recreation, etc. They need to feel free to discuss openly their insights and feelings about these matters. If they cannot share on this level, how can they ever share on deeper, more personal issues? However, a marriage will never become very intimate if the sharing stops here.

The sharing moves to a deeper level when the couple reveal their inner selves to one another: their thoughts and feelings about life and about who they are and who they wish to become; their convictions and their doubts about politics, God, death, and the afterlife; their priorities and their moral principles; their feelings toward one another; what is going on inside them in their various dealings with other people and in their diverse experiences of life. The more a couple are able to share of themselves on this level, the more they come to know and accept each other in intimate communion.

Sharing Decisions. The area of decision-making is crucial in a marital relationship. Most of us have a strong desire to control our lives and the environment that affects us. We wish to be captains of our own destiny. On the other hand, when we marry we desire to bind our lives together and to become in some way one. These two opposing desires are in tension when we come to decision-making. How we balance these in the decision-making process has significant impact on our marital happiness and intimacy.

There are at least three areas of decisions within the marriage. First, there are major decisions that affect the entire household (e.g., where to live, buying a house, family vacations, expenditures involving large sums of money). Second, there is an entire realm of less dramatic decisions that involve the family (such as menus for family meals, recreational plans, distribution of chores). Finally there are each person's individual decisions that, nevertheless, at least indirectly affect the rest of the family (how much to moonlight, how to dress, whether or not to smoke, whether to join the parish choir).

Obviously, a different level of sharing is called for in each of these areas of decision. Major decisions directly affecting the couple and the entire household deserve the free and open discussion of both spouses. Decisions in such matters ought to involve the consensus of both persons. Situations in which one partner "lays down the law," while the other is opposed, do not contribute to growing intimacy.

Within the whole scope of less important decisions that affect the entire household, a couple may wish to discuss the broad outlines, and delegate diverse details to each other. They need to make a continued effort to assure that both remain satisfied with agreed-upon arrangements.

In the realm of personal decisions that indirectly affect other members of the family, spouses ought to allow as much freedom as reasonable. At the same time each partner ought to consider the impact their personal decisions have on the other and be sensitive to the other's feelings. Even some of these kinds of decisions deserve appropriate consultation.

Enjoying Each Other's Company. There is obviously no mathematical correlation between the amount of time a couple are physically present to each other and the degree of intimacy they achieve. (After all, some couples spend a great deal of time fighting, arguing, and yelling at each other.) There is, however, a definite relationship between the time a couple spend together in the enjoyment of each other's company and the bonding process.

What does it mean to enjoy each other's company? Several things come to mind. The couple like being together. They get a real personal lift out of each other's companionship. They have fun together, even when the activity is as simple as taking a walk. They have developed a good sense of humor and a playfulness with one another.

The key word in all of this is enjoyment. Too many people have tended to approach life, and hence marriage, as work rather than enjoyment. The American ethos has contributed to this. Being in many ways a workaholic society, we have tended to bring that into the marriage. While it is true that we need to work at a marriage, it is also true that if we have to work too hard at it, it must not be working. Perhaps instead of working more at a marriage, many of us need to *play* more in our marriage and to enjoy each other's presence a great deal more than we do.

Shared Interests. An integral part of an intimate relationship is the couple's ability to share their hobbies, interests, and recreational diversions. In this area of their lives a couple need to achieve a balance and avoid two extremes. On the one hand they avoid living almost separate lives as far as their interests are concerned. One example of that extreme is the husband who pursues his hunting, fishing, and football while his wife spends her leisure time watching soaps, going to musicals, and playing bridge. Neither interferes with the other. Nor do they share their interests with one another. Once we called a friend. Her husband informed us she was away. When we inquired when she might return, he replied: "I have no idea. She lives her life, I live mine. We don't keep track of each other."

On the other hand, the opposite extreme of doing everything together can also block genuine intimacy. Resentment rather than growing unity results if one spouse feels forced by the other to participate in a lot of "recreational activities" that are of no personal interest.

A couple achieve a good balance in sharing interests and hobbies when they gladly share a number of activities together, and yet are free to pursue certain individual interests on their own. One couple illustrate this well. Fran enjoys swimming, likes to watch tennis matches, and has a particular interest in ballet, opera, and visiting art museums. Ed jogs, is a football and horse racing fan, and likes to travel. Ed occasionally joins Fran at the pool. Once in a while she jogs along with him. They not only encourage each other's interests, but often join one another in participating in the various fine arts performances and sports events. Ed appreciates the fact that under Fran's influence he has become exposed to good art and music. Fran has developed a greater taste for travel and has learned the basics operative on the football field and at the race track. Most important of all, their complementary interests have drawn them closer together.

Romance. Many of the things already spoken of in this chapter are part of maintaining the romance in a marriage. Three particular items especially pertain to keeping married life romantic: dating, surprises, and love notes.

While in our culture it is assumed that dating is essential in the premarital period, there is a tendency to overlook its importance throughout the life of the marriage. Dating is romantic. The couple take time out for one another, dress up in a special way, and celebrate their relationship by sharing in meaningful ways. Food, drink, and entertainment are an integral part of the date. However, the most significant elements of dating are the happy times together and the unforgettable memories. Dating is a potent way of keeping the marriage together, and of deepening the couple's romantic involvement with one another. Regardless of how busy they are, or how tight the budget, married partners need to invest the time and money to invite each other on dates, whether the date be an evening out, a weekend together, or a trip to the art museum.

When we speak of surprise in a romantic marriage, we are referring to unexpected expressions of love that tell in a special way of the tenderness and warmth which a spouse feels for the other. Whether it is a bouquet of flowers, a box of candy, tickets to the ballet or a football game, or a favorite dish that *he* cooked, it is the unexpectedness that gives it the special meaning. There was no particular reason or occasion for the "gift" except that you wanted to say "I love you" and knew that it would make your spouse happy.

Any couple who have saved the love notes they exchanged in their premarital days know that they probably would never express themselves in the exact same way today. As love deepens and is tested, much of the sugariness of earlier expressions tend to disappear. However, there continues to be a place for love notes. People never tire of being told that they are loved. Occasionally writing it gives further credibility to our saying it. Whether it is left on the pillow, or in the lunch bag, or sent to the office or factory, a special card or note communicating our love adds an important romantic touch.

Mutually Satisfying Sex Life. While sex alone certainly will not make or sustain the marriage, it is obviously an essential part of marital intimacy. Sexual intercourse can mean many things besides love. Some of its meanings (exploitation, conquest, mere selfishness) are absolutely opposed to the creation of intimate bonding between two people.

There is an obvious link between sexual intercourse and having children. It has taken a much longer time for society and for the churches to see that there is also a basic link between sexual intercourse and the ongoing intimate bonding of a married couple. One of the challenges to married couples today is to come to a deeper appreciation of the value of sexual intercourse for bringing them closer to each other, and hence closer to God, whose love is symbolized in married love. This calls for very positive attitudes toward the opposite sex. It also demands a generous giving of ourselves sexually to one another in ways that nurture the totality of our beings. The type of sexual sharing that fosters intimacy is deeply linked with all the other ways we are being for one another in the totality of our lives together.

Independence and Dependence. In a truly intimate marriage two people are interdependent and yet remain unique individuals. Neither loses her/his identity, nor becomes overpowered by the other. In fact, it is precisely in terms of their increasing unity that both are enabled to become enhanced as individuals.

There are at least three dimensions of our married lives in which it is helpful for our interdependence to be balanced by a healthy independence. The first is life management. In marriage we blend our daily lives together and divide many of the responsibilities that are related to survival and to the enrichment of life. In doing so it is important that each be able to be self-sufficient and not overly reliant on the other. While tasks are divided, both ought to be able to maintain a domicile, to cook, write checks, and put gasoline, water and oil in the car.

A second area is our social life. While our married partner becomes our best friend, and while we share each other's friends, each of us ought also to develop our own social circle. There is something inadequate if the only friends I have are those of my spouse. Good friends enrich our lives and make us better, more interesting people. Accordingly, healthy friendships strengthen our marriage.

A third dimension of our married life where it is important to balance interdependence with autonomy is in the economic area. Even during periods of the marriage where only one person is working, it is important that both have the skills and resources necessary to be self-supporting. This has impact on one's self-image. It also gives the couple flexibility in weathering the stress of unforeseen circumstances such as unemployment, financial crisis, and illness.

A balanced integration of dependence and autonomy not only serves the health of the marriage, it also prepares each of the couple for the life one of them must face when the other is gone. It is sad to see a widow who doesn't know how to write her first check for her husband's funeral, or a widower who can hardly boil water. It is tragic if after the death of a spouse the surviving spouse closes in on her/his little world. The best marriages are between people who have enough inner resources to make it on their own.

Summary

Marital intimacy is a lifelong process that involves commitment on the part of both wife and husband to share as much of themselves as possible with each other. In an authentic marital union, neither person surrenders her/his self-identity. Rather, each becomes enhanced as a unique individual precisely in terms of their growing intimacy.

Reflection Exercises

For All Readers

How do you evaluate the degree of authentic intimacy in each of the three marriages described at the beginning of this chapter?

For The Married

To what degree have you and your spouse achieved each of the characteristics of marital intimacy described in this chapter?

What areas deserve further attention?

What five concrete actions might help improve intimacy in your life?

For The Engaged

List the ten characteristics of marital intimacy treated in this chapter in what you each consider their order of importance. Compare your lists.

Select the two areas of intimacy that you think might be the most difficult for you to achieve in your future marriage.

What do you consider the main obstacles in each of these areas?

What three actions might improve intimacy in each of these two areas?

Chapter 3

Two for Dialogue

If asked what is the most important thing a couple must do to work toward marital intimacy, the answer would have to be: *communicate, communicate, communicate.* In this chapter we outline several important guidelines for good communication in marriage. While this chapter focuses on communication between spouses, the principles outlined here have application to other situations including communication with our children, our parents, and our friends.

1. Be in Possession of Yourself

In common parlance we speak of certain people being quite self-possessed. Basically, the way we are using the term here, self-possession includes three things: knowing who you are; feeling good about who you are; being so secure in your self-identity that you are not threatened by what other people think. Let us examine each of these components.

First, in order to reveal myself to another I must know myself. I must be in honest touch with the person I am. I must be able to communicate with myself if I am ever going to be able to communicate in an honest and open way with my spouse.

This kind of self-knowledge requires looking profoundly into the "mirror" and seeing the deeper "me," with all my strengths and weaknesses, talents and limitations, my virtues as well as my faults, and my realistic potential as well as what lies outside my realm of possibility.

It is not easy for most of us to embrace this kind of self-knowledge. We all have certain "blind spots" that prevent us from seeing ourselves as we truly are. We even "nurture" these blind spots so as to shield ourselves from whatever is too painful for us to face in our self-image. Once we can dare face ourselves in truthfulness, we are freed to allow our spouse to see us as we are. This enables us to communicate to our partner dimensions of our inner self that we ordinarily protect from public view. It also prepares us to accept insights into our darker as well as our brighter side that our spouse is in a position to impart.

A second component of self-possession is feeling good about yourself. Ironically, despite the fact that humanity is the crown of material creation, so many humans feel badly about themselves. We have been preoccupied with "original sin" and have neglected what Matthew Fox calls the "original blessing." We have felt so guilty about being sinners that we have rejoiced too little about being redeemed. We have concentrated so much on our "blemishes" that we have overlooked our uniqueness.

Such negative feelings about self block communication. Who wants to communicate a pessimistic view of oneself? Only if we feel good about ourselves will we believe we have something worthwhile to communicate to our spouse. Building a self-image that will make us feel good about ourselves is a long and continuous task. For some people the road is easier because they had parents who believed in them, loved them and accepted them. For others, rejection, non-acceptance, or various forms of psychological and physical abuse have created an almost insuperable barrier to joyful self-acceptance. We can build up our self-esteem by reflecting on God's love for us and on the value our loved ones and our friends see in us. Chapter 1 elaborated on the ways a person can improve her/his self-image.

The greater the self-esteem we have, the better we feel about communicating our inner self to our spouse. In turn, our spouse's reception of our self-communication affirms the good feelings we have about ourselves.

The third component of self-possession is inner security. This sense of personal security obviously flows from being in touch with oneself and feeling good about oneself. A person who has achieved a basic inner security is free to communicate her/his ideas, though someone might think they are foolish. She is free to share her feelings, though someone might ridicule them. She is free to reveal herself, though she might be rejected. Persons with inner security know that they will always land on their own two feet, regardless of what others think.

If prior to marriage the dating couple notice they have a communication problem, they would do well to examine the degree of self-possession they each have. If this is lacking, they need to find ways to improve their self-knowledge, their self-esteem, and their inner security. Otherwise, they will bring their communication problem right into their marriage.

2. Engage in Dialogue, not Monologue

The dialogue appropriate in marriage is conversation that takes place between two mature adults. In order for dialogue to happen in a marriage, both spouses must be willing and able (a) to communicate, (b) to listen, (c) to respond, and (d) to create an atmosphere in which both are able to engage in the discourse from an equal stance. Dialogue, therefore, is different from monologue. In monologue one person dominates the conversation in a way that makes it impossible for the other to be an equal participant. Let us examine each component of our definition of marital dialogue.

(a) Both spouses must be willing and able to *communicate.* It takes two to dialogue. Regardless of how willing and how skilled in communication arts one partner might be, there will be no quality communication in the marriage unless the other partner somehow matches this willingness and skill.

Both partners have to want to achieve deep, personal communication in their marriage. They have to make this a mutual priority. If one wishes intimate communication and the other is indifferent or apathetic, there is a complete impasse.

The willingness needs to be matched by skills. Some people would like to communicate, but find themselves unable to do so. This incapacity could be due to shyness, fear of rejection, or the fact that good communication was never modeled at home. If the willingness is there, the skills can be learned. A patient, understanding and communicative spouse can be an excellent teacher. A good book or workshop on the topic may also prove helpful. If professional counseling is called for, one ought not be ashamed. Where the couple are willing to work together, the desire and commitment to communicate can ordinarily overcome the barriers.

(b) Both spouses must be willing and able to *listen* to one another. Sometimes it happens that the people who are most willing and best able to talk are by that very fact least willing and capable of listening. Listening, of course, is essential to communication. Nothing you say is communicated unless someone is receiving it. For communication to take place in a marriage, there must always be a listener as well as a communicator. Otherwise, no contact is made.

Listening first involves hearing what one's spouse is saying. This means I ought to be able to repeat, at least for myself, the main ideas that have been communicated. When our youngest daughter thinks we have not really been listening to her, she will immediately ask: "What did I just say?"

Listening also involves understanding what my spouse meant by the words used. We ought not to make assumptions. Rather, we ought to make sure we know exactly what our spouse is saying. "I'm not sure I understand the point you are making. What do you mean by your last statement?" Or, "Why did you say what you just said?" Sometimes feedback is a good means of clarification. "This is what I hear you saying. . . . Do I understand you correctly?"

Listening includes letting your spouse know you appreciate the importance of what is being said. "I value what you wish to communicate, because it is important to you."

Listening is being attentive to the other person. It is taking your spouse seriously. It is being personally present to one another in every conversation. Good listening involves being sensitive to body language, being able to "read between the lines" and to sense the unspoken.

(c) Both spouses must be willing to *respond* to one another. Perhaps nothing is more frustrating than to express an opinion, describe an event, or share a feeling, and then receive no reaction from the person with whom we are trying to converse. Such non-response is insulting, for it makes you feel that you do not count as a person. It sends a loud message that what you think and how you feel are really of no consequence.

In order to create and maintain dialogue, it is essential to give meaningful response to what your spouse is communicating. You need to express interest in what is important to your spouse, affirm what you agree with, and manifest your disagreement. Above all you have to show that what your spouse says has some impact on you.

However, if you expect your spouse to be responsive, you must provide an environment that makes response possible. You need to invite response, ask questions and show interest in your partner's reactions. Some people so monopolize the conversation that they never give an opportunity for any meaningful response.

(d) Both spouses must work at *creating an atmosphere* that enables them to engage in the discourse from an equal stance. Basically such an atmosphere is created by treating one another as mature adults and by looking upon the other as someone from whom we need to learn. We then can perceive dialogue as important because our spouse is someone who will be able to correct our errors, balance the narrowness of our views, and open to us new horizons of vision.

If we are to be successful in allowing one another to participate in dialogue from an equal stance, there is a list of don'ts that deserves meticulous attention. Three head the list.

Avoid putdowns. "You're so stupid, how would you know anyway?"

Avoid sarcasms. "Another one of your *brilliant* ideas!" "With brains like that, you'll *really* go places."

Avoid being patronizing. Don't act as if you are the learned one who will deign to impart to your "ignorant" spouse some gems of wisdom. Some years ago at a party a male acquaintance of ours was engaging in such an exercise with his spouse. He then turned to us and, measuring with his hand, proclaimed: "You only bring them up this high, and no higher."

Communicating, listening, responding, and treating each other as equals: these are four of the ingredients that make authentic dialogue possible.

3. Make the Time; Choose the Opportune Moment

In the Greek language there are two words for time. *Chronos* refers to the time of day; *kairos* means the opportune moment. To establish good communication in marriage, we must be attentive to both aspects of time.

First, we must make sure that we have enough time to communicate on a regular basis. Because of the busyness of our lives, and the hectic schedule of our jobs, the routine management of the household, and caring for our children, most of us find that we have to make some kind of conscious effort if we are to communicate regularly in some depth. For many this effort means making sure that daily, or at least frequently, we have time to be alone together, without the distractions of television, busy chores, and the demands of children.

The other aspect of time that is relevant to good communication is choosing the opportune moment. This is especially true of topics that might take a lot of concentration, or a lot of time to discuss, and topics that might be very emotionally charged. Perhaps two guidelines are particularly relevant. First, if you bring up a topic that will require thought and time to discuss thoroughly, choose a time slot when both are relatively fresh and free of distractions. The last moments before dinner when the pots and pans on all four burners need immediate attention is not the time to discuss plans for the family vacation. When you are both ready to collapse at night is not the proper moment to start discussing whether you should send your children to a different school.

Second, if there is a topic that is potentially explosive, bring it up at a time when there is greatest hope that it can be dealt with more effectively and more calmly. If your spouse is already tired and depressed, this might not be the time to tell him how much his father's drinking bothers you. When you are so angry that you can hardly speak rationally, maybe you need to cool down before you "enter into dialogue." Ordinarily, at meals we ought to avoid those topics that could stir up a lot of hard feelings and hence obstruct good digestion and turn the table into a battleground.

4. Be Honest—but in the Spirit of Love

The ideal in good communication is for the couple to be straightforward with one another. On the negative side this means not telling lies to each other. Such dishonesty obviously breaks down trust. However, bold-faced lying is not the only way to violate honesty. Playing with the truth in ways that are deliberately intended to mislead the other is in conflict with honest communication.

On the positive side, being honest means being open with each other. We have already spoken elsewhere about the need to reveal ourselves to our spouse. However, we are often asked the question, "Does this mean you have to tell your spouse everything, under every circumstance?" Our answer to this question is that self-revelation, important though it be, is not the ultimate virtue. Love is. While we ought to be as open as we can with our spouse, this openness must serve the purpose of building a bond of trust and friendship between us.

This brings up two practical questions. The first is: "Do I need to share all my opinions with my spouse?" When it helps build the relationship, yes. But if the only purpose to be served by telling my spouse how awful his father looked in those pants is to cause hard feeling and create a fight, why say it?

The second question is more complex. What about those "skeletons in the closet": the isolated homosexual experience he had when he was fifteen; the abortion she had when she was seventeen; the affair he was involved in six years ago; the baby she birthed and gave up for adoption while in high school? "Should I share these secrets?" There is no simple answer to which of these kinds of secrets one ought to reveal to one's future or present spouse. Certainly one does not have "to go to confession" to one's spouse, telling all one's "sins." Some matters, however, are better revealed. The only thing we can do here is to suggest some guidelines that might help a person make the decision about when or whether to reveal a particular "skeleton" from the past.

(a) If some secret of this nature is to be revealed to someone with whom you are serious, it is better, we believe, that it be revealed prior to the marriage, even, preferably, prior to the engagement. Waiting until after the marriage can raise questions about trust: "Why didn't you tell me sooner?" "Couldn't you trust me?"

(b) If it is possible that your future spouse could learn about the secret from another source, then tell her/him. It is much better to find out from you rather than from someone else. This will also allay fears you might have as you wonder if and when your spouse will discover your secret.

(c) If you cannot bear to hold this secret from someone you intend to marry, and it will make you feel better within yourself and in the relationship to reveal it, then do so.

(d) If, however, none of the above pertains, and there is no other advantage to you, your spouse or the relationship in revealing the "skeleton," and all it could do is cause unnecessary harm, then you need to ask yourself why you would reveal this.

If you do decide you ought to reveal such a secret, you may fear that your projected spouse might reject you. Perhaps the best answer here is that if this person cannot accept you as you are, and cannot understand and forgive, then it is better to know this now, rather than later.

5. Share Your Feelings

Even people who may have little or no problem dialoguing about their ideas and opinions often find it difficult to communicate their feelings. There are at least three reasons for the reluctance to communicate honestly one's personal feelings. First, our society has tended to downgrade feelings. Feelings were seen to be a sign of weakness.

"Mature adults don't let their feelings get in the way." "Approach things rationally," that is, dispassionately, cerebrally. Because of its sexist stereotype, society condescendingly "allowed" women to cry and demonstrate their feelings, since it falsely accused women of being "the weaker sex" anyway. Even then, demonstrative women were often looked upon as being "hysterical." Men, on the other hand, were always supposed to be "in control." In such a negative climate, it is no wonder that many people, especially men, are disinclined to show their feelings.

A second obstacle to manifesting emotions comes from the "religious" training to which many people were exposed. The emotions of anger, fear, jealousy were looked upon as wrong. They were vices to be avoided. Often, people were not taught to make the distinction between a righteous anger and the "sin" of anger, or between a justified jealousy and a wrong kind of jealousy. Many people felt guilty about even feeling these emotions, and consequently tried to repress them. The non-biblical and erroneous image of "the meek and humble Jesus" became the model for dispassionate behavior.

A third reason why many people find it difficult to express their feelings is because it is risky. When I put my emotions "on the table," I make myself very vulnerable. If someone is already shy by nature, such a risk might be almost impossible to take.

In order for good communication of feelings to take place in marriage we need to be able to do three things: (a) we have to accept our feelings; (b) we need to be expressive of our feelings; (c) we need to give affirmative response to each other's feelings.

(a) *We need to accept our feelings.* We have to believe that it is all right to have feelings. We are inspirited bodies, embodied spirits. Hence, we are not only physically affected by our surroundings, we are also psychologically and spiritually affected. To be emotional, then, is an integral part of our human mode of existence.

The emotions that many people find the hardest to accept are fear, anger, and the hurt that leads to crying. We need to convince ourselves that it is all right to feel these emotions. Feeling afraid is not the same as being weak, or cowardly, or "a scaredy cat." Feeling angry is not the same as being violent. Crying because of hurt, sadness, or out of sentiment is not the same as being "thin-skinned" or "a sissy." The experience of these emotions often depends on the depth of our convictions and the degree of maturity and sensitivity one has achieved. We can be proud of the ability to have strong feelings. The only thing wrong with feelings is allowing them to lead us to inhuman rather than to human behavior.

(b) *We need to be expressive of our feelings.* Since our emotional makeup is an integral part of who we are, the expression of our emotions is an essential element of our self-revelation to our spouse.

There are really two major groups of emotions. There are emotions that make us feel good, such as love, a sense of well-being, a feeling of pride, joy, gratitude. Then there are emotions that disturb and upset us: for example, anger, frustration, annoyance, a feeling of disappointment, fear, jealousy, anxiety, depression, sadness.

We may neglect communicating the first set of emotions, those that make us feel good, either because through laziness we just don't bother making the effort, or because we believe those feelings ought to be obvious to our spouse and, hence, expressing them is rather superfluous.

Expressing such emotions is important. The very saying of the words reinforces the feelings. To say "I love you," and mean it, deepens the love. Saying "thank you" strengthens our sense of gratitude. Expressing these emotions is always reassuring to the other person. One's actions can always be misinterpreted. Honestly saying "I love you," "I am really grateful for all you do," clarifies how I feel. Such verbal communication helps the other to interpret correctly my actions and my facial expressions. Without honest, clarifying words, deeds and looks can be ambiguous. Finally, expressing our good feelings is important because it creates an environment that fosters personal intimacy. If we communicate frequently our emotions of love, gratitude and joy, we make the other person feel loved, appreciated and happy. Such communication also evokes from our spouse similar expressions of affection and gratitude.

Communicating the second group of emotions, those that disturb and upset us, poses a different set of difficulties. I may not wish to communicate my anger or disappointment because I don't want to hurt your feelings. If I express my fears, I might look weak. Telling you how depressed I feel might make you feel bad. On top of all that may be the cynical attitude, "What good does it do anyway to tell someone how you feel?" "Who cares?"

But if we do not explicitly and clearly communicate these kinds of emotions, they will still manifest themselves in other "hidden" ways (such as pouting, hostile body language, silence). This will confuse our spouse and block the development of an intimate relationship. A mature expression of such emotions is highly therapeutic. Often, just telling another how we feel has a soothing, calming effect, and enables us to put the situation that disturbs us into proper perspective.

Since expressing feelings of anger, fear and jealousy

is particularly problematic, a few reflections on handling and communicating each of these emotions is in order.

Anger. It is important to assess how and why we get angry. Do I get angry often or infrequently? Am I a "slow-burner" or do I "fly off the handle" quickly? Is my anger usually due to my own bad moods or to things others have done? At whom am I angry: my spouse, my children, or someone else? If I am angry at my spouse, is it due to minor irritations (the burnt toast, the pots and pans put back in the wrong place), or to a spouse's serious infractions (overdrinking, continued refusal to help with household chores, flirting with others)?

When we feel angry just because we are in a plain bad mood, or because of something that someone other than our spouse has done, we ought to let our spouse know that we are angry and why. "I'm just in a horrible mood today, but it has nothing to do with anything you have done." "The children are really driving me buggy today." "I can't stand the sight of my boss. He is a pompous, hypocritical overachiever." Expressing this kind of anger to our spouse helps get the anger out of our system. It also clears the air so that our spouse knows that our anger is not directed at her/him.

When it is our spouse whom we are angry at, we need to proceed with discernment and measure our actions according to the annoyance. Is the matter of such a nature that it is worth making an issue over it? Maybe I am initially irritated because my spouse forgot on a particular occasion to turn off the dining room light. Why get nasty about it? Smile, turn it off, and be done with it. If the lights are always being left on, then, instead of exploding, say as pleasantly as possible, "I get annoyed at the way you so often leave the lights on. Do you think you could try to remember to turn them off?"

When the matter is more serious, a more firm expression of anger is called for. There is a place for raising one's voice and pounding the table to get a point across. There is no place, however, for physical abuse and name-calling. What is said in the following sections in this chapter on constructive criticism and fair fighting will address further how we ought to express deep anger over serious matters.

In all expressions of anger "I" statements are preferable to "you" statements. Statements such as "I get irritated when you don't put your dirty dishes in the dishwasher," "I am angry and concerned about the amount of alcohol you are drinking," are less accusatory and less threatening than "Your sloppiness in the kitchen drives me crazy," "Your drunkenness makes me sick." "I" statements are an honest and accurate account of how I feel. They express my ownership of my angry feelings and leave the door open for dialogue. "You" statements attack and put the other on the defensive, and hence often close the door to productive discussion.

Jealousy. This is another emotion which most people immediately regard in a disparaging way. While some modes of jealousy are irrationally based, other forms of jealousy are very legitimate. Webster's Dictionary helps us distinguish between these different kinds of jealousy. To be jealous is to be "intolerant of rivalry or unfaithfulness," "disposed to suspect rivalry or unfaithfulness: apprehensive of the loss of another's exclusive devotion," "hostile toward a rival or one believed to enjoy an advantage," "vigilant in guarding a possession," "distrustfully watchful."

Operating out of some of these forms of jealousy would be detrimental to a marital relationship. Guarding one's wife as a possession is based on a false and unhealthy premise. Regarding one's spouse as a rival whom

I cannot permit to get ahead of me is contradictory to the view of marriage as a partnership.

Other forms of jealousy are ambiguous. "Distrustful watchfulness" over a spouse who has never given any grounds for suspicion is far different from distrustful watchfulness over one who has had affairs. Being "intolerant of rivalry or unfaithfulness" and being "apprehensive of the loss of another's exclusive devotion" can be reasonable or unreasonable depending on what we mean by "faithfulness" and by "exclusive devotion."

The very meaning of the marital covenant presupposes a permanent commitment to a unique level of personal intimacy and sexual expression that is exclusive of everyone but one's spouse. Fidelity to this commitment and exclusivity is to be expected and demanded. The area of intimacy unique to marriage is to be "jealously guarded." Feelings of "reasonable jealousy" are to be communicated clearly and firmly when a spouse has acted in any one of a variety of ways in which fidelity to the marital covenant can be compromised.

Besides the reasonable feelings of jealousy that ought to be experienced under certain circumstances, many people are prone to at least occasional irrational jealous feelings. One should not do hostile actions based on these feelings. Sometimes it may help to discuss even these kinds of irrational feelings with one's spouse.

Fear. It is natural for all of us to have certain fears. Being limited creatures we are vulnerable to any variety of mishaps and tragedies. Hence, we cannot avoid thinking about the possibility of fire, earthquake, nuclear attack, the loss of a loved one, cancer, "early" death. If we thought about these possibilities long enough, we could allow ourselves to become petrified.

We need to acknowledge our fears and to try to perceive as far as possible why we are afraid. We also need to distinguish reasonable fears from irrational ones, take intelligent means to avoid the evils we fear, and learn to cope with our irrational fears.

Georgina's parents were both heavy smokers who died in their fifties of lung cancer. Hence, it is reasonable that one of the things Georgina fears the most is lung cancer. Rather than becoming obsessed with the fear, she took two constructive actions: she moved to a less polluted city, and she gave up smoking. Then she went on with her life.

Ralph would be the first to admit that his refusal to ride in small planes is irrational. Commercial airliners are fine, but he will never get in a small, private plane. He not only acknowledges his fear, he also knows its origin. When he was eighteen, a plane crashed two hundred yards away from him, killing both passengers. He and his wife have talked about this. She respects his fear. Once they were both invited to tour the city in a friend's small plane. With mutual consent, his wife flew, while he stayed home—and prayed!

(c) *We need to give affirmative response to one another's feelings.* Accepting feelings with empathy nurtures the other's being. It enables each of us to "be me," so we can be right for ourselves and for others. All the suggestions for accepting our feelings and for communicating them fall flat if our spouse creates a negative environment that makes such communication embarrassing, painful or futile. Everytime Helen would go into tears, Larry headed for the local bar. Whenever Bernie told Louise of his fear of dying of a sudden heart attack as his father had, Mary berated him for being a hypochondriac. Irene discovered that when she told Ron she was angry at something he had done, he exploded and read to her a litany of the things he didn't like about her. All of these kinds of responses cut the communication right off and leave the partner feeling worse. Such responses also discourage expression of emotions on future occasions.

If we wish to create a marital environment that fosters and encourages a free and open expression of emotions, there are some don'ts and some do's.

Don't blame. People cannot help feeling the way they feel. Therefore, we should not accuse and judge them because of the way they feel.

Don't ridicule. Name-calling and insulting remarks manifest a clear rejection of the person's feelings and make it almost impossible for a person to be honest in communicating her/his emotions.

Don't ignore. Nothing is more frustrating than to pour your feelings out and then have the other person stare ahead, shrug, say nothing, or abruptly change the subject.

Don't patronize—as if you, the strong partner, are so great to tolerate your "weaker" partner's feelings. If we're honest we know we too have vulnerable feelings, so let's not act as if we don't.

Don't act like the "know it all." "I know how you feel." "I understand what you are going through." Could anyone possibly know how another person really feels? It's better to have this attitude: "I haven't walked this path or been in this situation, so you'll have to tell *me* how you feel."

Don't lecture. Clichés like "cheer up," "snap out of it," will not console someone who is depressed. Such sayings will probably plunge the person more deeply into melancholy, because they manifest so great a lack of sensitivity and understanding.

Do listen. Give your spouse plenty of time to express

how s/he feels and why. Do plenty of listening before you do a lot of talking.

Enter into your spouse's feelings. Try to feel what s/he feels. Have empathy.

Let your body language speak before your mouth does. Our body position, facial expression, and body attentiveness, a touch, an embrace speak much more loudly and effectively than words.

6. Criticize Constructively

To many people the word "criticism" means an unfavorable remark. This, indeed, is part of Webster's definition: "the act of criticizing, esp. unfavorably." However, that is only part of the definition. The second meaning of the word criticism that Webster gives is at least as important: "The art of judging with knowledge and propriety the beauties and faults of works of art or literature; hence, similar consideration of moral or logical values." When we speak here of spouses engaging in constructive criticism of one another we have in mind the second meaning of the word, and wish to apply that to the marital situation. Doing so we come up with this definition of constructive criticism between spouses: it is the *art* whereby spouses *judge* with *knowledge* and *propriety* the *beauties* as well as the *faults* of one another. Let's explore each of the underlined words in this definition.

Constructive criticism is an *art*. So, it takes skill, practice, and ingenuity. Anyone can complain, "blast out" at another, or flatter someone. It takes a great deal of delicacy, sensitivity and a proper sense of timing to express a judgment of another in ways that will enlighten, heal, encourage and inspire the other to improve, or to keep up the good work.

One of our favorite examples of criticism as an art is the spouse who came home from work and smelled her husband's rolls beginning to burn in the oven. Instead of saying—as so many of us would—"The rolls are burning," or, worse, "*You're* burning the rolls," she gracefully took a few sniffs and pleasantly said: "Mmm! How nice! I see we're having rolls for dinner." Immediately her husband remembered the rolls and raced to the oven!

Constructive criticism involves making a *judgment.* "Well," someone will say, "we're not supposed to make judgments. After all, the Bible says, 'Judge not and you shall not be judged.' " Such a remark reflects the mentality that reduces the word "judgment" to the word "condemnation." We ought to avoid condemning people and imputing motives. We must, however, have opinions of people and make decisions in their regard. Spouses ought not condemn one another, but they do need at times to express their opinion of one another.

Constructive criticism is given with *knowledge.* We ought to criticize from all of the knowledge we have about the person. Our words need to express accurately what we know. We need to refrain from proclaiming what we don't know.

Constructive criticism is engaged in with *propriety,* that is, with common courtesy, and with regard for the other. We can correct without insulting. We can criticize an action without denigrating the person. We can cure what's wrong without inflicting needless wounds.

Constructive criticism judges the *beauties* as well as the *faults* of one another. Presumably, people who fall in love and marry saw more beauty in each other than blemishes. It is important that we never lose sight of the beauty. Too often amidst the daily routine of maintaining a household together, couples can allow the irritating faults to blind them from all the goodness in each other.

In a marriage, constructive criticism ought to be centered far more on the beauties than on the faults. A couple need to affirm frequently each other's talents, virtues and accomplishments. Sincere praise should flow easily and abundantly. When faults and mistakes have to be pointed out, this should be done in the context of our overall appreciation of the good things we see in our spouse.

7. "Fight" Fairly

The term "fight" is used here in quotation marks because the common understanding of the word includes elements that are inappropriate in an intimate marriage. Soldiers fight in battle to kill. Boxers fight to win over an opponent by injuring or knocking the person into unconsciousness. Obviously, there ought to be no room in a good marriage for physical or psychological abuse. Hopefully, even when things get volatile and there are serious issues to work out, spouses will still consider themselves partners and not opponents. It is important that in confrontations, one spouse doesn't try to claim victory. It may be a cliché, but one worth repeating: "If one spouse wins, they both lose." The other's dignity or self respect is shaken or s/he is made to feel of little or no account.

One might ask, "Why, then, are you discussing marital 'fighting' if you are excluding several elements that are ordinarily associated with the term?" Because even in the best of marriages there will be occasions of heated dispute, squabbles, unhappy confrontation. Most couples refer to these incidents as "fights." These "fights" can either become nasty (and habitual) encounters that erode the relationship, or they can be occasional occurrences that can "clear the air" and are integrated into the ongoing well-being and growth of the marriage. Since these incidents involve expressions of anger and criticism, what was said on these two topics above apply here. A few further considerations come to mind.

Keep "fights" to a minimum. Many situations can be handled in more peaceful ways.

Keep your attention and your remarks focused on the precise point about which you are fighting. Don't drag in all the other faults your spouse has.

As much as possible, "fight" in private. "Fighting" in front of the children can be very disturbing, even frightening, to them.

"Fighting" before friends ought also to be avoided. It causes everybody unnecessary embarrassment.

Don't run away from a "fight," letting it just hang there. Bring it to conclusion.

Don't go to sleep angry. Have some way of making up before sleep sets in.

Summary

Obviously the topic of communication has to pervade an entire book on marriage. The first two chapters of this book imply good marital communication. All of the topics treated in the subsequent chapters involve the same.

Marriages are built or broken on the basis of the quality of the communication couples choose. Because of this centrality, the present chapter focused explicitly and directly on the topic. Being in possession of oneself, the willingness to enter into authentic dialogue and effort to take the time are key requisites for communication to take place. Honesty in love is the most foundational virtue that needs to pervade all marital communication, even the most delicate and problematic areas of sharing one's feelings, criticizing one's spouse, or engaging in fair "fighting."

While we conclude our formal treatment of communication, we hardly leave the topic. Perhaps there is no dimension of the marriage where communication is more essential than in the area of sexuality, the topic of the next chapter.

Reflection Exercises

For All Readers

Do you think you have good, fair or poor self-esteem? Why?

How does your degree of self-esteem affect the way you communicate to others?

Do you find it easy or difficult to express your feelings? Why?

How were feelings expressed in your family when you were being raised?

How does this family environment influence the way you now express (or don't express) feelings?

How do you handle criticism that you receive from others?

What would be some good guidelines for receiving constructive criticism gracefully?

For Married Couples

The chapter outlines four major components for authentic dialogue. How well do you think you have achieved each of these components of dialogue in your marriage?

Which specific feelings do you have the greatest difficulty expressing to each other? Why?

Are there some concrete ways in which you could help each other express these feelings?

In your relationship, do you find that you affirm the beauties in each other much more than you point out the faults? Explain.

When you do point out faults in each other, what elements that make criticism constructive are present, and which are absent?

What can you do to make your criticism more constructive?

Have you ever "fought" in your marriage?

If so, how often, and over what issues?

In what ways did you "fight" fairly, and in what ways were you unfair?

What three things do you consider would be most helpful in improving your communication with each other?

For Engaged Couples

Are there any "skeletons in your closet"?

If so, how have you decided to communicate (or not communicate) these to your fiancé(e)? Why?

In your courtship have you experienced feelings of anger and/or jealousy in regard to each other?

If so, what occasioned these feelings?

In your estimation how well did you handle and communicate these feelings? Check your answer with your fiancé(e).

As you read over the entire chapter, what aspects of good communication do you think are already present to a high degree in your relationship?

In what ways can these be nurtured even further?

What aspects of good communication do you identify as missing or quite defective in your relationship?

What concrete means are you going to take to improve these?

Do you have any fears about achieving and maintaining a good level of communication in your marriage? If so, what are they?

How can you together now address these fears?

Chapter 4

Sexual Intimacy

The expression of love in sexual intercourse is an integral part of marital intimacy. Intercourse, however, has many meanings. It can comfort or sadden, unite or alienate, enrich or devastate.

How can sexuality be approached in marriage, so as to build a unique relationship between the couple, rather than be a block to their growth in personal intimacy? In addressing this question we first explore the meaning of sexuality and sexual intimacy. We then reflect on some aspects of the sexual relationship in marriage. Finally, we consider the topic of premarital sexual preparation.

Human Sexuality

The young man sat in the counseling room, discouraged and down on himself. "Here I am, only twenty-nine, and I have been through two marriages, two divorces and eleven affairs, yet I have nothing to show for it. I am alone, and have no one. I have found plenty of sex, but have never discovered love."

The experience of this man underscores the fact that sex and love are not necessarily intertwined. Humans must make free choices about their sex life. Sex is not something that just happens to them. Through our free choices we determine the meaning that sex has in regard to our personal growth and the development of personal relationships.

It is this freedom of choice that distinguishes human sexuality from sexuality in the rest of the animal kingdom. Humans are not driven by blind instinct. They are not victims of uncontrollable sexual urges. They must choose what they wish to do with their sexuality and what meaning sexual experience will have for them.

In general, we have three major options regarding how we choose to engage in the genital expression of sex: indulge in sex merely as a means of recreation; use sex in ways that exploit other people; channel our sexual energies and drives toward a committed, loving, lasting relationship with one person.

The casual use of sex in many circles today underscores the allurement that sex for recreation has. "Sex is fun," the student observed. "What's wrong with having a little fun, as long as both people agree?" The problem is that such a choice is made at the price of foregoing personal commitment, fidelity and love.

Exploitative sex is another option open to us. Sexual exploitation is using someone sexually for one's own self-centered purposes, regardless of what destructive effect this might have on the other. Prostitution, rape and sexual abuse, pornography, and much advertising are clear examples of such exploitation. Sexual exploitation is dropping someone after you have gotten what you want sexually. It is using a person as a sexual object.

What is unique to us as humans is our ability to know, to love, and to enter into bonding and lasting relationships. Sexuality is expressed in a human way to the degree in which we know and love the other, and are committed to an enduring relationship. To the degree these qualities are lacking, sexuality is less than human.

In a good marriage sexual expression takes on its fullest meaning. There are many aspects to the significance that sexual intercourse can have in an intimate marriage. Here we reflect on eight of them.

1. In intercourse the couple present themselves to each other in their physical *nakedness*. They reveal themselves as they are. Nothing external is hidden. This physical nakedness before one another is symbolic of the desire they have to reveal to each other their inner selves, in all of their spiritual "nakedness."

2. There is no way for a couple to achieve any greater physical *closeness* than in sexual intercourse. Through this physical closeness, they enter into emotional, psychological, and spiritual closeness. This sexual intimacy celebrates and nurtures the intimacy of their whole married life.

3. The couple give of themselves in sexual intercourse for the *enjoyment* of one another. The enjoyment they experience in intercourse catches up the other moments of joy in their marriage, and intensifies those moments.

4. In sexual intercourse the couple not only give and do for one another, they *are for one another*. They bask in the intimacy of each other's presence. The experience of being for one another in intercourse makes the couple more sensitive to the beauty and transforming power of personal presence. This experience can color how they relate to one another in the rest of their marriage. They learn to slow down and take time to be with one another. They discover that it is not necessary to be always doing something for one another.

5. The married couple in sexual intercourse show their *appreciation* for each other. They are "saying" through their sexual intimacy: "I find you attractive." "I like being with you." "You are the most important human in my life." This celebration of their mutual appreciation in intercourse leads them to show appreciation for one another in the other aspects of their married life.

6. The exclusive giving of oneself to one's spouse in sexual intercourse is an act of *faith* and *trust*. They express their belief in one another and in each other's love. There is belief that "I mean as much to you as you mean to me." There is faith that "you will be there for me tomorrow, as you are today."

7. Marital intercourse expresses the couple's acceptance of each other as *equals* who relate "on equal ground." In intercourse the couple meet one another in the depth of their basic humanness, in their human commonality. This presupposes that they have already acknowledged one another as equals in their relationship. The experience of commonality in intercourse will deepen their awareness and acknowledgement of equality and oneness in all of the dimensions of their marriage.

8. Sexual intercourse is an expression of *reconciliation* and the serious intent to grow in personal unity. Even the best of marriages has its stresses and strains. In sexual intercourse the couple express their desire not to allow the failings to create a barrier to their growing intimacy. They express sorrow and forgiveness. They show their determination to work beyond the hurts, and to continue to grow toward oneness.

Dispelling the Misconceptions

The misconceptions about sexuality that some people bring to a marriage can block sexual intimacy. The following five exemplify some of the more common misconceptions.

1. *Sex, if not "dirty," is at least tainted.* This impression has been burned deeply into the consciousness of many. Two quite opposing groups have specially fostered, even if unwittingly, the perception of sex as tainted: the pornography industry, and the Church.

The pornography industry portrays sex as violent, lustful, insensitive and abusive of women and children. The correct response to pornography is revulsion and disgust.

Coming from an entirely opposite direction, the Catholic Church has also been a powerful influence in shaping negative views about sex. It has done so, first, through an excessive preoccupation with sexual sins. While Jesus' teaching concentrated on love for all humans, and compassionate concern for the needy, the focus of the Church's most rigid moral teaching has been on sexual sins. According to this teaching, one could commit "venial sins" in matters of lying, stealing and the physical abuse of others, but the slightest deliberate indulgence in sexual pleasure "outside of marriage" was a "mortal sin."

The Church has also fostered negative attitudes toward sexuality and marriage by its bias in favor of celibacy. This bias is seen, for example, in the exaltation of Mary more for being "ever virgin" than for being a married woman of faith. The long litany of women saints is dominated by "virgins." The relatively few married women among the saints made the list as "widows." This bias against marriage has obscured many of the beautiful and positive things the Church has had to say during the past twenty-five years in regard to married life.

Against this background of negativity, it is understandable that many experience difficulty feeling good about their sexuality and freely enjoying the sexual pleasures of marital intercourse. However, through their open communication with each other and their experience of the personal growth that comes from tender and loving sexual experiences, the couple can gradually learn to put aside negative impressions and feelings about sex.

2. *Men are supposed to be sexually aggressive, while women are to be passive.* This misconception has been fed by cultural stereotypes. According to the stereotypes, the male is "macho-man," who, almost beside himself with sexual passion, is on the prowl to conquer his "female prey." The female's role, in the stereotype, is to submit passively to "her man's passions." Her enjoyment is "to give him pleasure." The stereotype even perceives her as "enjoying it" when he is violent and rapes her.

One can easily perceive how dangerous these misconceived stereotypes are. They can have a number of damaging effects on the efforts to establish sexual intimacy in marriage. They warp one's perspective in regard to the opposite sex and to the nature of heterosexual relationships. They block one from discovering a partner as a unique other and instead lead one to see the partner through the prism of the stereotype.

The stereotype of husband as initiator and wife as passive submitter puts unnecessary pressure on the husband "to perform," and places unjust pressure on the wife to submit and endure all sorts of possible abuses that are intolerable in a marital relationship. The stereotype is also blind to the sexual drives, energies and "assertiveness" of the woman. Finally, it obstructs mutual initiative and enjoyment, and prevents the partners from experiencing each other as persons who are equal in human dignity and deserving of the same respect and treatment.

3. *Good sex will make a good marriage.* There are at least two ways in which this misconception can operate. It can lead a couple before marriage to believe that because they have an intense sexual involvement, they are in love, and united in mind and heart. Blinded by their sexual infatuation, they may not think it necessary to step back and take a good look at each other and reflect on the element of compatibility and incompatibility in their total relationship. They may not realize that an enduring, satisfying sex life flows from personal intimacy. Knowing and loving the other and getting along well in married life do not necessarily flow from "good" sexual encounters.

This misconception can also lead to the illusion that a good sex life will automatically solve problems. Instead of confronting a drinking problem, or facing together the issue that caused a serious dispute, the couple may be led to "bury" the difficulty, or to "drown" the pain by sexual intercourse. It is true that marital intercourse can play a very important role in the process whereby a couple work through a difficulty, and become reconciled after hurt and pain. But in order for intercourse to have this healing effect, it must take place within the framework of the broader process of consciously and honestly facing the problem and working it out. Sexual intercourse provides no easy escape from that task.

4. *Sex is always a "super" experience.* Despite this common misconception that somehow sex is always going to be an extraordinary, almost ecstatic experience, sexual intercourse shares in the plight of all human experiences. They are limited, dependent on mood, and on a variety of

changing conditions and circumstances. To expect every sexual encounter "to reach the heights" is obviously an illusion, and is bound to lead to disappointment. Relatively few sexual experiences will be "five star." Some will be "one star," and most will fall somewhere in between the two.

5. *Married people are always "ready for sex."* This misconception may be due in part to what is experienced in the courtship situation. When a couple who are serious about each other date, they often experience an almost irresistible sexual attraction for one another. If they have decided not to engage in premarital intercourse, they realize what a struggle this can entail. From this experience a person might come to think that married couples are always in the mood for a sexual encounter. Courtship, however, is different from marriage. In the dating situation the couple see each other at choice times: they usually look their best, are exhilarated to be together again, and are unencumbered from other demands and distractions. In marriage the couple journey together through all the diverse moments, good and bad, that make up married life. They see each other at their best and at their worst. They struggle to find time for each other in the midst of the demands of supporting the family, maintaining a household, and caring for the children. While, indeed, in a loving marriage a couple grow in sexual intimacy, this takes place within the rhythm of the entire marital reality.

Creating Sexual Intimacy

Taking seriously the true meaning of human sexuality, and correcting any misconceptions one might have, will serve as an important foundation for a healthy sex life in marriage. Beyond that, a couple can work at ensuring the presence of several elements in their sexual encounters that will make a significant contribution toward creating sexual intimacy.

Communication. Perhaps one of the most difficult topics for a couple to talk about is their sex life. Because the topic is so personal, some are embarrassed to discuss it. And since it is such a sensitive issue, spouses may be very reluctant to criticize one another and make suggestions that might improve their sexual experience. Hence, it is very tempting to bury the topic and endure the status quo.

One woman explained her silence this way: "He goes into a long pout if I even criticize his table manners. You can just imagine how he would react if I criticized how he acts in bed." One husband observed: "It's stupid to talk about how you make love. You just do it. Who needs all those discussions and books?"

While it may be difficult, it is also crucial for a couple to discuss honestly how they are experiencing their sexual encounters. They need to be able to express how they feel, what they like and what they don't like, what is bringing satisfaction and what is causing dissatisfaction or hurt. They need to be able to guide and direct each other. They ought to create an atmosphere in which both are free to communicate these feelings before, during and after intercourse.

Mutual Respect and Regard. A couple's respect for the dignity and uniqueness of each other reflects itself in sexual matters. They respect each other's conscience about the moral aspects of sexual behavior and have regard for what each finds tasteful or distasteful. They are sensitive to one another's moods and physical states. They refrain from exerting undue pressure on one another, and come to decisions about sexual matters through mutual agreement.

Variety. Like everything else in life, marital intercourse could become routine and mechanical. The most basic way to keep marital intercourse alive, new and exciting, is to instill continually into the relationship new life and excitement. In order for romance to be preserved in marital intercourse, it must be kept in the entirety of the marriage.

More specifically, variety can also be achieved by changing, at least occasionally, the immediate environment in which lovemaking takes place. Diversifying the time, location, or technique from time to time can help prevent routine. Variety can also be enhanced by candlelight, flowers, music or a night away.

Another way of bringing variety into lovemaking is to enter into the different moods of each other at the time of lovemaking. Entering fully into the distinctive spirit of the other, be it playfulness and joy or discouragement or grief, gives a very particular and memorable tone to individual encounters. Such variety prevents routine and boredom and provides a rich and meaningful diversity to the couple's sex life.

Sense of Humor. There is a human tendency to take ourselves too seriously. Sometimes we become over-sensitive to criticism and too touchy. One place where this tendency could easily manifest itself is in sexual intercourse. One of the remedies to all of this is to lighten up and enjoy. Couples need to be able to laugh at themselves and see that we humans really are sort of funny creatures. They need to be able to view in a lighter vein some of their foibles and shortcomings, and to see the humorous dimensions in human lovemaking.

Going Beyond the Biological. The difficulty with

many "how to" manuals on sexual intercourse is that they concentrate heavily, if not exclusively, on physical "techniques" and the biological aspects of the act. Obviously, the physical aspects cannot be overlooked, and some "techniques" can be helpful. However, complete mastery of these alone will never bring lasting satisfaction. Unless attention is also given to the psychological and spiritual aspects of sexual intercourse, sexual encounters will ultimately leave the couple emotionally and spiritually starved.

Sexual yearnings are an expression of our far deeper yearnings for love and for personal union. The best way for a couple to enhance their sex life is to become intimate lovers in all of the dimensions of the ordinary realities that comprise married life. As this happens, a couple become increasingly capable of sensing and responding in intercourse to each other's emotional and spiritual yearnings, as well as to their physical desires. Sensitivity, gentleness, caring, and the willingness to reveal to each other our deeper selves are qualities that, if present in the marriage and in sexual intercourse, will greatly enhance the sexual experience. These qualities will enable the couple to touch, through the physical contact of intercourse, the profounder dimensions of one another's being.

Sensitivity Toward Difficulties

Creating sexual intimacy will not be without at least some occasional difficulties. In some marriages the problems may be of a sufficiently serious nature that expert counseling or therapy may be required. In most marital relationships the occasional sexual difficulties are average enough that they can usually be worked out by the couple themselves, if the total picture of their marriage is a healthy one, and if the couple are able to discuss frankly the matter with sensitivity and encouragement. We include here just a few examples of the kind of moderate difficulties that could occur, at least occasionally, in the course of just about any marriage.

Frequency. During various periods of the marriage one partner may experience notably more intense sexual desire than the other. Accordingly one may wish to make love much more frequently than one's partner. Such a difference could become a real battleground if one starts engaging in name-calling, or begins making accusations ("You don't love me anymore." "Are you seeing someone else?"). The situation is also aggravated by trying to put one's partner on a guilt trip ("After all I do for you, this is the least you can do for me"), or by making authoritarian demands ("This is my right, and your duty!"). On the other hand, a mutually satisfactory compromise could be reached if there is calm discussion in which both partners try, in a non-judgmental way, to understand and appreciate where each other is in this regard.

Premature Male Orgasm. Foreplay is an integral and indispensable part of lovemaking. It helps situate sexual intercourse in an environment of tenderness, fun and mutual excitement. It prepares both partners psychologically and physically. It also involves the art of timing. Both partners try somehow to synchronize the pace and rhythm of their sexual excitement. Achieving a mutually satisfactory tempo does not come automatically. So, it is very possible, especially in the beginning of a relationship, that the male may reach climax before he has penetrated. This can be frustrating for the female partner and perhaps embarrassing for the male. Disappointment could easily lead to anger. If both partners, however, are sensitive to one another, they can work this difficulty out in a constructive way. The husband ought to be concerned about his wife achieving some kind of satisfaction. The couple can then discuss ways of better synchronizing in the future.

Temporary Impotency. It is within the realm of "normal" experience for a male, either on a given occasion or for a period of time, to be unable to have an erection or to maintain one in the course of lovemaking. The environment of the marital relationship has a great deal to do with how well a couple can work through a situation of temporary impotency. Negative reactions on the part of one's spouse can only increase anxiety over the matter. The anxiety, in turn, aggravates the impotency. On the other hand, understanding, support, and patience, along with honest dialogue, are often all that is needed to deal successfully with this problem.

Temporary Frigidity. This term refers to the inability of a woman to achieve orgasm over a limited time period. There can be a number of reasons for this. It can be due to psychological or physical conditions. Is enough foreplay taking place for both to be adequately prepared for intercourse? Are there difficulties in the marriage that might be interfering with the woman's experience of lovemaking?

Again, as in the case of other sexual difficulties, understanding, sensitivity and communication are the first keys for addressing this problem. Sometimes the couple can work through the difficulty themselves. At other times counseling might prove helpful. Certainly, frigidity ought not be ignored and allowed to persist indefinitely.

Planning Conception

Though the emphasis so far in this chapter has been on the relational dimensions of sexuality, obviously sexual intercourse is also intrinsically linked by its nature to the conception of new human life. Responsible sexual intimacy must have regard and concern for this aspect of sexual intercourse and assume responsibility for it. Decisions in this regard must be made jointly by the couple. In doing so, a couple must dialogue honestly and openly about where each stands in regard to the main issues involved: desire for children, moral, aesthetical and risk aspects of various methods of family planning, and the question of who will be responsible.

Desire for Children. Even before marriage, it is imperative that a couple discuss at some length how they feel about having children. They may need to face some serious questions. Do they want to have children in their marriage? If so, how many, and according to what time frame? Both partners need to satisfy themselves that their views on these questions are compatible. The impossibility of reaching some mutually agreeable compromise on these issues ought to forewarn the couple that they have not yet found a suitable partner. The earlier this is discovered in the premarital relationship, the better for all concerned.

Moral Aspects. It can no longer be assumed that two people belonging to the same religious denomination hold similar views regarding what is moral or immoral in the matter of family planning. Sociological surveys have shown, for example, that approximately seventy-five percent of Catholics disagree with the official Roman Catholic position on birth control. Hence, even if both partners are of the same religious persuasion, it is necessary for them to discuss their moral perspectives on a variety of questions: Is natural family planning the only permissible form of contraception? Are all forms of artificial birth control acceptable, including abortifacients? Are sterilizations ever permissible? What about the morality of abortion?

Divergences in a couple's convictions in regard to these issues need to be addressed. Both partners have to respect the conscience of one another.

Aesthetical Aspects. Every method of contraception, "natural" or "artificial," involves some inconvenience, and often interferes to some degree with spontaneity. In choosing a means of contraception, a couple need to discuss which method both of them find least unaesthetical.

Risk Aspects. Some methods of contraception carry with them a risk factor. These ought to be carefully weighed. It ought also be noted that many of the greatest risks are connected with contraceptives used by women.

The Responsibility Factor. In our male dominated society, it has too frequently been assumed that contraception is the woman's responsibility. "It's her fault that she got pregnant. She should have done something to prevent it." The couple need, in fairness, to be co-responsible for family planning. It is unjust to let the burden fall on the woman because the male doesn't want to be bothered.

Premarital Sexuality

Preparing for sexual intimacy in marriage does not begin on the wedding day, but in the developmental years prior to marriage. What one does with one's sexuality in these years has implications for one's marriage. Hence, before we conclude this chapter we wish to take up the topic of premarital sexuality.

High school and college religion teachers are used to being besieged with the question, "Do you think it's all right to engage in premarital sex?" There are two serious problems with the way this question is asked. First, the term "premarital sex" is too broad. It is essential to clarify what the person using the words has in mind. Second, the questioner usually wants an answer in terms of whether or not "it is a mortal sin." Addressing the question merely in this way often overlooks many of the other important aspects of the issue.

We are concerned in our treatment of premarital sexuality in this book with the effects the various forms of premarital sexuality can have on the person involved and on a future marriage. Hence, we will address the topic by dealing individually with several forms of premarital sex.

Joe was sixteen when he had his first encounter with a prostitute. During his last two years of college his visits averaged twice a month. He wondered what effect this might have on his future marriage.

While no one can predict the answer to that question, a couple of concerns come to mind that go beyond the obvious one of possible disease. The first concern is about the attitude toward sex and toward women that is manifested in males hiring prostitutes for sexual services. In the dynamic of prostitution the male purchases the sexual use and service of a woman for a price. The prostitute is subservient to the demands and wishes of the male. Authentic love, sensitivity, and consideration have no place in the package. Male concern for what is and will happen to the prostitute is almost non-existent.

Is a person like Joe going to be able to abandon easily

the attitude toward sex and toward women that is imbedded in his past practice? Or will these attitudes be brought into the marriage and tinge the way he relates to his wife? Will the habit of divorcing sex from love affect his marital sexual encounters and be an obstacle in achieving true sexual intimacy with his spouse?

The second concern has to do with the addictive element in lust (i.e., sex without love). In his sexual purchases, Joe has had genital entanglement with many different kinds of women. He has also had available to him all sorts of "kinky" behavior that are not part of most marital relationships. Will the appetite that Joe has built up reappear after the "first excitement" of marriage has died down? This question takes on deeper significance in light of studies and media interviews with certain prostitutes that reveal that a high percentage of the men engaging the services of prostitutes are married!

Another form of premarital sexual experience is the "one night stand." "Why pay for it?" Walt commented. "There are enough people out there willing to go to bed. All you have to do is look for them." While "one night stands" do not share in all of the evil attached to prostitution, this practice bodes poorly for a future marriage. It involves using people sexually, and then dropping them. It can also whet the appetite for a variety of partners, thus making marital fidelity a more difficult goal to achieve. It is a serious mistake to think that all these attractions will automatically disappear after marriage. "I'll have my fun now and settle down after marriage" may be much easier said than done.

Rachel had always rejected "one night stands." Her story exemplifies another form of premarital sex. She would only go to bed with someone for whom she "cared" and for whom she "had some feeling." This led her, during her late teens and early twenties, through four affairs, each ranging from three months to a year. What she discovered was: "Two of the men never really loved me. All they were doing was using me. The remaining two, on the other hand, did care. It just didn't work out."

Rachel's story reflects two very distinct kinds of experiences of premarital affairs. In two of the affairs, Rachel believed her partner shared the same feelings for her that she had for him. When she discovered otherwise, she felt used and abused. There is an evil of sexual exploitation in this kind of experience that is missing from her other two affairs, where both she and her lovers did have some care and feeling for each other. While this distinction does not make the second kind of affair morally right, it does make it morally different. Further, one who has sexually exploited others is certainly less prepared for marriage than one who has not.

A final major category of premarital sex is the sexual involvement of two persons who are engaged to one another. They are in love, are committed to each other, and have set a date for the wedding. "We are all but married, except for the piece of paper. Waiting has become almost impossible. What is wrong with having sexual intercourse in these circumstances?"

The authors of this book are traditional enough to continue to maintain that the most meaningful and, hence, ideal context for sexual intercourse is marriage. However, the reality is that a growing number of people do not share this view. Is there any guidance that can be given to an engaged couple who are determined in their consciences that for them "premarital sexual intercourse is all right"? Does one just say flatly, "I disagree"? Or does one help them at least to face certain questions that might clarify for them their situation? The latter seems the more helpful approach.

Here are some of the questions an engaged couple who have decided to have sexual intercourse before marriage would do well to consider: If we already "feel married," why don't we get married now? Do the reasons we give for delaying marriage outweigh the reasons for marrying now? Do we both feel the same way about postponing the marriage? If so, do we both have the same reasons? Does sexual intercourse have similar meaning for both of us in terms of our love and our exclusive permanent commitment toward each other? Have we discussed and agreed upon a course of action in the event of premarital pregnancy? Are we economically independent, or is one person pretty much financially supporting the other at this point in time? Have we achieved a degree of good communication and intimacy in the other areas of our relationship that is commensurate with the physical intimacy expressed in bed?

Honestly addressing such questions together enables the couple to see where each is coming from in regard to their decision. It protects against the possibility of one person taking advantage of the other.

Whatever one wants to say about the morality of an engaged couple having premarital intercourse, this issue needs to be kept separate from other forms of premarital sex. It is very unhelpful and unrealistic to put all the diverse forms of sexual activity just described under the one heading "premarital sex" and then to treat them on equal moral footing. It is much more useful to help people see the specific characteristics that are at work in their sexual involvement, and to assess what effect this involvement is having on them, their partner, and their future marriage.

Summary

The sexual expression of love finds its most meaningful context in marriage. Sexual intimacy, however, does not happen automatically. The quality of marital intercourse is related to the degree of intimacy achieved in all the other areas of the couple's relationship.

Sexual intercourse has many meanings and a variety of moods. By exploring these meanings, being open to these diverse moods, and bringing the total gift of themselves to their lovemaking, a couple can experience the richness of marital intercourse and achieve true sexual intimacy. In light of a positive understanding and experience of sexuality, misconceptions regarding sex can be corrected and problem areas can be constructively addressed.

Reflection Exercises

For All Readers

Have you ever been influenced by any of the misconceptions about sexuality referred to in this chapter?
With which insights in regard to the meaning of sexuality discussed in this chapter do you agree?
With which ones do you disagree?
What is your own opinion in regard to premarital sexual activity?

SEXUAL INTIMACY

For Married Couples

The authors reflect on eight aspects of the significance that sexual intercourse can have. How do you experience these meanings in your own sexual intimacy?

A number of ways of creating sexual intimacy are suggested in this chapter. Which of these have you already achieved to a satisfactory level in your relationship?

Which need improvement?

Are there some concrete things you can do to bring about this improvement?

Have you confronted any problem areas in your sexual relationship? If so, how have you addressed these?

For Engaged Couples

What are the points of agreement and/or disagreement between you and your fiancé(e) in regard to:
(1) the number of children you would like to have, and how you would like to space them;
(2) the moral, aesthetical and risk aspects of various methods of family planning;
(3) what means of family planning you intend to pursue?

What decision did the both of you reach in regard to premarital sexual activity? How did you reach this decision, and for what reasons? In what ways are you comfortable and in what ways are you uncomfortable with this decision?

Chapter 5

Co-Parenting

In dealing with this topic we address two basic questions. What attitudes toward parenting and toward each other make for good partnership in parenting? How can the couple work together in the ongoing process of nurturing that includes caring, discipline and the total formation of the child?

Changing Attitudes

In stereotyping and distributing roles in regard to parenting, patriarchal society carved out a niche most convenient for the father—at the distinctive expense of the mother. The father, in this stereotype, fulfilled his paternal duties by working outside the home, earning money to support the family, and being the chief disciplinarian. Fathers who went "beyond the call of duty" also taught their sons how to play ball and how to become "men." In this model, the question was never raised—as it always is for women—about how a man can balance his outside job with his parenting. His power to earn money was seen as an essential element of his role as father. Almost all of the parental responsibilities were assigned to the mother.

Since she bore the child, it was assumed that most of the responsibility for raising the child belonged to her also. She was the one expected to get up with the baby at night, prepare all the meals, change the diapers, and look after the baby twenty-four hours a day. On top of all this, her efforts merited very little respect, and were often taken for granted. "I don't know what the big hassle is," one man commented some time ago. "I have to get out and work; all she has to do is sit home all day with the baby."

Thanks to the feminist movement, the consciousness of both women and men has been raised during the past two decades, and many have come to see how inadequate and unfair that stereotyped view of parenthood is. Mothers, fathers, and children were all, to some degree, losers in that arrangement.

In this section of the chapter, we would like to identify several of the important attitudes that are crucial in order for both partners to work together and help each other bring to their joint venture of parenting the best of what is mother and father in each of them.

1. *The marriage comes first; parenting second.* This would seem like an obvious fact. However, it hasn't been quite a quarter of a century since the Catholic Church abandoned the position it held, for over a millennium and a half, that the primary purpose of marriage was the procreation of children, while the spousal relationship was secondary. It is only in the past few decades that society has gotten over the erroneous thinking that even the worst of marriages ought to be "kept together" for the "sake of the children." And still today one will find a couple who think they can solve their marital problems by having a child. "A child," that misthinking goes, "will help cement our relationship."

All of these forms of thinking put parenting before

the marriage. In the first form, parenting was more important than the marriage. Marriage existed for the sake of parenting, rather than the latter flowing from the former. In the second, the basic peace and happiness of individuals trapped in an intolerable relationship was to be sacrificed at the altar of parenthood. In the third, a magic power is attributed to parenting as if it could cure the difficulties in a marriage that the couple themselves had not been able to address.

The quality of the marital relationship must be the first focus of the couple. They cannot enter into the joint venture of nurturing their children if they have not entered into the joint venture of nurturing each other. They cannot welcome their children into their community if they have not established community—communion—with one another. They cannot give their children the experience of what marital love and trust are about if they have not been able to build a bond of affection and belief in one another.

Contemporary psychology shows that the first gift that a couple can give their child is their love for one another. The love, warmth and happiness they experience for each another creates an environment in which the child finds acceptance and security. Children, in turn, have an effect on the marriage. If there is love and communication between the couple, children can indeed enhance the marital relationship. The mutual commitment to parenting becomes another significant area of sharing that binds the couple even more closely together.

2. *For the couple with children, parenting ought to be the next highest priority after their marriage.* This statement, of course, flies in the face of much that is imbedded in our American culture and economic system. Success is identified with how high one climbs the career

ladder and with how much money one makes. Parenting, on the other hand, is very much a "hidden" enterprise that brings little recognition and certainly no financial recompense.

Hence, a couple really have to examine their scale of values. Do we measure our "success" as human beings more in terms of career promotions and money than in terms of the efforts we have made at parenting? Or do we believe that after our marriage, parenting is the most important contribution we make? It is our firm belief that if a couple has children, then the couple should take care of those children.

3. *Parenting is just as much a responsibility of the father as it is of the mother.* The best model for parenting is co-parenting. Together the couple assume parenting as a joint enterprise. They bring together the best of who they are as parents, and in cooperation nurture their children through their personal presence, their affection and the sharing of themselves.

Co-parenting means we do not allow sexist stereotypes to determine the distribution of parental chores. It is the authors' strong conviction that both fathers and mothers must willingly assume their fair share of all the menial tasks involved in parenting: changing diapers, feeding the baby, caring for the ill child at three in the morning. Statistical studies show that the vast majority of mothers—including those who have jobs outside the home—are still expected to assume all these tasks. An increasing number of fathers, however, are doing their share, and discovering that this is increasing their bond with the children.

It is also important for fathers to take on, occasionally at least, babysitting responsibilities for a whole day, a weekend, or perhaps an entire week, while mother is given the opportunity to "get away from it all." This does wonders for both the marital as well as the parental relationships. It also gives the male a new understanding and appreciation of the challenges as well as the joys of spending long periods of time alone with small children.

4. *In parenting, the giving is not one way, but two ways.* Too often people talk of the responsibilities of parenthood and of all that parents give to their children. Not enough attention is given to what children—including infants and babies—do for the parents. We often think of children as having "to be raised." We tend to treat them as "adults-to-be," as the "future generation." This way of thinking denigrates the importance of children as children. Precisely because our young offspring are children, they have something important to offer us.

Parenting, then, is not just a matter of teaching the child. It also involves learning from the child. Parenting cannot be a monologue. It is rather the entrance into dialogue with the child and the child's world. It is this that can enrich the couple as adults and indeed enhance their marriage.

Affirming Self-Image

The greatest gift we can give our children is to help them acquire a good image of themselves and an authentic self-love. A child who possesses this gift is equipped for life to withstand peer pressure, to confront the bully, and to develop the good s/he sees in herself/himself.

But how can parents help nurture rather than damage a child's self-image? Several guidelines are worthy of consideration.

It is imperative to accept and love the child as s/he

is. Authentic love, Louis Evely wrote, is to bid someone to live, to invite her to grow. A real joy of parenting is to wait and discover who your child is in her/his uniqueness. The temptation to impose our preconceived notion of what *we* want the child to be must be resisted. When it is not resisted, it is to the detriment of the child.

While, indeed, we want the best for our children, we ought to want what is truly best *for them,* and not what we think is best. We should want them to become all they are called to be, but not something else.

Comparing a child to siblings or other "model children" has to be avoided. A friend once confided, "When I was growing up I heard so much from my parents about my cousin, Len, I really got to hate him. Everytime I did anything wrong, they told me how much he helped his mother, how obedient he was, and what high grades he got in school." Such comparisons are devastating. Each child has to be dealt with on her/his own ground. Where improvement is needed, the point of comparison ought to be the child's own greater potential, not someone else's accomplishment. And where there is improvement, let's be sure to tell the child how far s/he has advanced from where she/he was.

Avoid trying to push a child beyond her/his capabilities. One of the more distressing sights is a father yelling epithets at his child who has just missed a shot in a CYO fourth grade basketball tournament. Why do some parents insist that their children must always win, or be number one, or that they get all A's? Such insistence puts tremendous pressure on the child, and is guaranteed to make the child feel horrible when s/he fails to live up to their expectations. One high school sophomore dreaded going home with his report card because he only got seven A's out of a possible eight. "I will be grounded for a week because of that one B." Our competitive world is taking its toll.

We need to affirm our children in what they are able to do and encourage them to do their best. We also need to help them accept their limitations and feel good about themselves. If a C average, or coming in twenty-fifth in the spelling bee, or winding up on the fourth string on the high school football team is the best a child can do, then parents ought to be satisfied and help the child to be content.

We ought not to treat each of our children alike, but as much as possible respond to the unique needs of each. According to an old misconception, parents were supposed to treat all of their children in the same way. This approach receives widespread support from most children, who are ever ready with outcries of "unfair" the moment one child gets what another doesn't.

Actually, treating each child alike is what could be very unfair. Each child has a unique set of needs, interests and talents that all ought to be addressed. Where fairness and the avoiding of favoritism come in is in trying to affirm the individuality of each child and to provide opportunities that encourage the development of a child's particular gifts and talents.

Discipline

Unfortunately, as soon as many people hear the word "discipline," they think of punishment or restriction. The word, however, comes from the Latin "disciplina," which means "teaching." This provides a key for approaching child discipline. It is a teaching and learning process. And precisely what is it that we wish a child to learn? Hopefully, we want her/him to learn to become a well-balanced, loving human being who can independently function in society. The first way parents contribute to this process is by being themselves well-balanced and loving humans and by treating their children as such.

Discipline, then, embraces much more than punishing and restricting. Further, any valid punishment or restriction ought to contribute to the child's learning how to become more fully human. Having said all this, several points need to be made about the matter of disciplining children.

Parents must be in basic agreement with each other in the discipline of their children. Even before the marriage, it is good for the couple to know something of how each other was reared, since that has deeply influenced attitudes toward discipline of one's own children. They need to be satisfied that in general their views in this area are compatible.

When they become parents, the couple ought to discuss their disciplinary policies and work out a common front. If one parent, for example, allows the children to eat junk food whenever they want, and the other forbids anything for snacks except fruit, vegetables and bread, the situation can become chaotic, and the children are left totally confused. They also begin to play one parent against the other. Such matters as when the children can bring friends over to the house, when they can begin to go to mixed parties, what time they must be home at night, are the kinds of things a couple ought to agree upon and then hold a common line.

When one parent punishes a child, the other ought never to reverse that punishment. If you think the punishment is unreasonable, talk privately with your spouse. If you both agree the punishment was too severe, let the parent who gave the punishment be the one to reduce it or take it away.

Agreement on policies and punishments enables the couple to support each other in dealing with the children. It also provides the children with a consistent and stable environment.

As they grow older, children can be given increasing opportunity to contribute input into disciplinary policies. When they have had some input, the policies will be more acceptable to the children. Moreover, they will feel more responsible to observe a decision with which they have agreed. Instead of announcing to the sixteen year old daughter at what hour she must be home from the movies, perhaps she could be asked what she considers a reasonable time. If you agree, you have avoided all hassle. If you disagree, there is room for reasonable compromise. Instead of proclaiming a punishment for a serious infraction, the parents can ask their child what she thinks would be a reasonable penalty. That can become the starting point for reaching an agreement on what all parties consider a just punishment.

Do not put your children in situations with which they are simply unable to cope. Many of the "fights" that offspring and parents get into could easily be avoided if parents did not make impossible demands on them. Are small children capable of sitting quietly in a doctor's waiting room for an hour? Do they belong in church "listening" to long sermons that most older people find boring? Adults need to be sensitive to the restless bodies of children and their short attention span.

Give some leeway in assigning deadlines for tasks and the obeying of orders. Here's another battleground: a parent wants the child to do a particular thing "right now"; the child wants to do it "in fifteen minutes," "three hours," "next week." Some things have to be done now; others can wait. Discerning and organized parents plan enough ahead so as to allow some option. For example, instead of waiting to the last minute and then shouting, "You must set the table now," a parent can give a forewarning, "You need to set the table within the next half-hour." This allows time for children to finish what they are doing and leaves them better disposed to cooperate.

Be flexibly consistent. This combination might seem contradictory to some. The intent, however, is to point toward a balanced approach that avoids both the extremes of a topsy-turvy unstable environment on the one hand, and an insensitive rigidity on the other.

In order for children to learn, they need to experience some kind of consistent pattern of behavior on the part of the parents. They need to know what kind of behavior is ordinarily acceptable and what kind is unacceptable. They also need to know the kind of consequences that will ensue.

Our discipline ought to be constructive, that is, it ought to build our children up rather than tear them down. There are three ways in which this can be accomplished.

First, we need to avoid constantly nagging and picking on our children for everything they do wrong. We have to discern when to correct and when to ignore.

Second, discipline (teaching) is not just a matter of being negative. It is, more significantly, a matter of being positive. If we teach what to be and what to do, there will be less need to harp on what not to do. Parents need to affirm their children's good behavior more than they criticize their undesirable behavior.

The third way in which discipline can be constructive is in the choice of appropriate punishment. So often when it comes to punishment, we immediately think in negative terms: take something nice away, forbid the child to do something s/he enjoys, deprive the child of a privilege. There is a place, of course, for these types of punishments. But with a little imagination, we could just as easily come up with something that is much more creative, corrective and healing. For example, instead of grounding a child or taking away TV, we can have the child do an extra chore or a kindness.

Don't threaten unreasonable punishments that will never be carried out. Is there a parent who has not "flown off the handle" and in anger threatened some punishment that is totally out of proportion with the "crime" and that s/he will never conceivably impose? The parent has "had it" with the sloppy way the children keep their room, or the way they fight "all the time." So, in anger, the proclamations fly: "There will be no more television in this house. I'm having it taken out." "You can kiss Santa Claus goodbye this year." "Since you kids can't get along, we'll cancel summer vacation."

Such demonstrations do let steam off, but they are obviously ineffective. The parents know they will never do this. The children know that the parents are "just on a rampage" and are not to be taken seriously. The only difficulty with all of this is it can lessen the parents' credibility, and lead the children to take the parents lightly even when they are serious.

Discipline should be free of violence. Americans are a people prone to violence. Violence, along with sex, is the most popular entertainment. The cries for capital punishment are increasing. Wife battering and child abuse are on the rise. No wonder, then, that when it comes to disciplining children, yelling, name-calling, and hitting are the first things to which many parents resort. They are also the very things that need to be avoided if our discipline is to teach children how to be loving, and how to handle difficult situations in a healing manner, rather than in destructive and violent ways.

Name-calling is dangerous because it can lead to violent action. The word can be "father" of the action. Calling a person bad names can lead to treating her/him badly. Violence begins in the mind and the heart. It is then expressed in word, and finally in deed.

When correcting children, it is important to make a clear distinction between the action and the person. The child's action may have been bad, or discourteous, or stupid. The child is none of these things. "I disapprove of your action, but I love you." Negative criticism of the wrongness of an action needs to be balanced by an affirming of the child's goodness. "What you did was wrong, but you are a good person."

What about spanking? Is it ever admissible? There are two opposing views. On the one side, some parents and experts say "A good spanking won't hurt anyone." The opposite view is that parents ought never to spank. Hitting a child is a violent act that both teaches violence and can lead to further abuse. The authors of this book are opposed to spanking in principle, and yet we confess that we have on occasion resorted to it when just about everything else seemed to fail.

The ideal, we believe, is never to hit a child. If you're in a position where you feel you must spank, a few guidelines are in order: (1) Never spank in anger. Spanking ought not be done as a release of temper. If it is done, it ought to be for the benefit of the child. (2) Do it only as a last resort. (3) Only spank on the rear end. (4) Keep the spanking within the minimum required to make your point.

These rules seem obvious. They can, however, be difficult to observe, especially when parents have been pushed to the limit of their power to cope.

When a parent has erred in a matter of discipline, the parent ought to quickly admit the mistake, apologize, and ask for the child's forgiveness. Some adults may be afraid to admit a mistake to a child because of the need "to save face" and to "keep the respect of the child." In a good parental relationship "saving face" ought not to be necessary. It is more important to treat children justly and with sensitivity.

Moreover, it is good for children to know that their parents are human, make mistakes, and have weaknesses and faults. It is also important that youngsters know that their parents are big enough to admit their errors and to make up for the hurt they have caused. Perhaps the most significant way in which children learn to say "I'm sorry" and "I forgive" is by experiencing this from their parents.

Parents need to withstand parental peer pressure. There has been a lot of talk about teenage peer pressure, but not enough about parent peer pressure. It's there and its real, and one's children will be the main vehicles of communicating it. "Cliff watches five hours of television a day." "Cindy's parents allowed her to have her ears pierced when she was only nine." "Vic's Dad let him have his own car when he was sixteen." "Jenny's mom lets her have teenage drinking parties when she's not home."

Some of the reports that children make about what other parents allow are exaggerated and self-serving. That aside, there is clear evidence that an alarming number of parents allow their children to get into situations that they cannot handle. Some parents are sponsoring mixed parties for eleven year olds and allowing unchaperoned spring breaks in Florida for fifteen year olds. All of this permissiveness exercises a lot of pressure on other children, and through them on their parents. Parents need the courage, the inner security, and the tough love necessary to stand their ground and allow what seems reasonable, and to forbid what seems hazardous to the well-being of their children.

Finally, all discipline and punishment ought to begin and end in a context of love. This refers first to the general context of the parent-child love relationship that hopefully develops throughout the years. It also refers to the specific love shown to the child during the course of a particular disciplinary action.

When we restrict a child's behavior we ought to explain our reasons and make clear we are doing so out of love and concern. When we need to impose a punishment, we ought to do so in a loving way. The best way for a disciplinary confrontation to end is in a kiss and a hug. This makes clear that our love is steadfast and is not dependent on a child's behavior.

Parents as Educators

The teachings of Vatican II give formal support to the fact that parents are their children's primary educators. This truth has particular application to three important aspects of the educational roles of parents: their relationship to the school; their responsibility for sex education; their task as religious educators.

Parents and Schools. The more deeply parents believe that they are the primary educators, the more easily they may become frustrated when they actually have to deal with school systems. For, though schools verbally proclaim the primary role of parents as educators, their policies are often geared to keep parents in their place. "We are the professionals," many educators are heard to say. "Who are parents to tell us what to do?" What many parents experience is that the input the schools want from them is threefold: pay, obey, and compel your children to fit into the system. When parents want a further role, that's when the sparks may begin to fly.

A basic question that must be faced by parents and educators is this: Are parents in the employ of the school and of the teachers, or are the school and the teachers in the employ of the parents? If the latter is true, we need to test our stand by asking further questions.

What say is given the parents as a whole (and not just the few on the parish or school board of education who too easily become the pawns of administrators) in the hiring, firing and annual assessment of principals and teachers? Are parents, for example, ever given evaluation forms in which they are invited to share their opinion of the strengths and weaknesses of the school personnel?

In what ways does the school solicit opinions of parents in regard to school policies that affect them (e.g., uniforms, changes in school schedule, the inauguration of seventh grade school dances)?

Are the Parent Teacher Associations or Organizations used as vehicles for fostering communication and dialogue, or merely as the means of raising money?

Are open houses and classroom visitations by parents encouraged?

Are sessions set up each semester in which teachers explain to parents the curriculum they are teaching, their homework policies, and ways in which parents can help the children?

The answers to these kinds of questions will indicate who really are considered the primary educators in a given school situation. Where parents' rights as educators are not being respected, parents should do all in their power to change the situation.

Sex Education. The most important sex education takes place in the home, and begins in the first couple of years of the child's life. Sex education is caught more than taught. It is caught first from the attitudes of the parents toward one another, toward sex, and toward the body. It is caught from the love and affection of the parents for one another and for their children. The deepest lesson children learn in a loving environment is that sex is linked to marriage and commitment, to love and life-giving, to respect and concern.

Sex education also takes place at home through discussion. The best policy here is to address sex matters in an open manner whenever and wherever they come up. No age, even two, is too young to receive honest answers to questions. Answer every question simply, to the point and on the level it is asked. Don't go into long dissertations about matters that are not asked. Use correct language and accurate descriptions. Forget the stork, and speak of the womb and not "mommy's tummy." Refer to the genitals and to all bodily functions by their proper names and not by euphemisms.

As children grow older (eight, ten, twelve and on) the discussion can become increasingly sophisticated. In our home the dinner table has just happened to become the principal place where discussions on sex have spontaneously emerged. Whatever topic is brought up by a child—sexual intercourse, rape, adultery, AIDS, teenage sex (and the related issues of drinking and drugs)—is discussed as long as the questions and the interest level continue. The topics are often occasioned by a TV show, a news report, or a school conversation. Such discussions often lead to ethical and aesthetic assessments—made first by the children, then picked up by the parents.

In sex education, strong emphasis needs to be put not only on the beauty and goodness of sex, but also on the child's right over her or his body. We need to convince children that their bodies belong to them and that they need to feel secure, and free to say no to any bodily intrusion, either of sex, or of alcohol, or of drugs. Everything that was said earlier about fostering a child's good self-image comes into play here.

Religious Education. Like sex education, religious education is also a matter which is much more caught than taught. The goal of parental religious education is to facilitate the growth of a child's life of faith and discipleship. Several things can be kept in mind as parents engage in this delicate enterprise.

1. *We cannot bring about faith in another person.* Only God can. Faith is a personal relationship with God that involves, first, the free gift of grace on the part of God, and second, the free response on the part of an individual. Both of these factors lie outside the control of a third party. Parents and educators need to resist the temptation of believing that somehow, if they only talk enough, or use persuasive arguments, or impose sufficient rules, they can create faith and a religious attitude in a child.

All parents can do is to create an environment that nurtures faith growth. They do this primarily by their own example, by sharing their faith insights with their children, and by praying with them.

2. *In order for parents to nurture the faith of their children, they need first to come to grips with their own faith.* It makes little sense to be concerned about the Christian development of our children, if Christianity means nothing to the parents. Hence, before becoming in-

volved with the religious growth of their children, parents do well to ask themselves a number of questions. What does it mean for me to be a baptized Christian? How do I experience Christ in my life? What does building the kingdom of God mean in our lives? What meaning does going to church on Sunday have for me? What is my experience of confirmation, Eucharist, and the sacrament of reconciliation?

Once we can identify the particular value that the various elements of Christian life have for us, we have a better idea of why we wish to pass them on to our children. We are also in a more enlightened position to explain to our children the meaning and value of the beliefs and practices that make up Christian discipleship.

3. *We need to be willing and able to discuss issues and address questions on religious matters as they come up, and on the level at which they are raised.* Such responses as "It's a mystery," "I'm not a theologian," and "You'll have to ask a priest" are cop-outs, and "put-offs." Dig into your own faith life and your own knowledge, and answer the question in simple terms that are commensurate with the way the question was asked, and with the age level of the child. Obviously, a question on death, for example, will be addressed differently when it comes from a two year old than when it is asked by an eleven year old. If there is a question that you can't answer, find out.

It is also important that we have some idea of what our children are learning in the school or church religion programs. Parents ought to be able to have some input into what goes on in these classes, and to integrate what is worthwhile in these programs with the ongoing religious formation in the home. Of the two, what takes place in the home is of greater significance for the child.

The child, especially under twelve, learns much more from religious experience than from technical, abstract dissertations about God and religion. We would do better to do a lot less talking to our children about God, and much more talking with our children to God.

Some of the points that will be raised in the last chapter on marriage and Christian discipleship will pertain further to the issue discussed here regarding the religious formation of our children.

Summary

Children can be a wonderful part of a happy marriage. How they affect the marriage will depend on the quality of the love relationship of their parents. In turn, the greatest gift that parents can give their children is the love they have for one another.

The call to married couples with children is to be co-parents. With matching commitment, the couple take seriously their parental responsibilities. They work together in creating a life-giving environment, and in ministering daily to the physical, emotional and spiritual needs of their children. They assume their role as the primary educators in the challenging task of enabling children to grow as well-adjusted, loving human beings, who, in turn, will be able to make a life-giving contribution to their own families and to the broader human community.

Reflection Exercises

For All Readers

What is your opinion of the authors' conviction that parenting is just as much the father's responsibility as it is the mother's?

Why is affirming a good self-image of a child so important?

What difference does it make in bringing up a child whether the parents approach discipline primarily as punishment or primarily as teaching?

In our society does calling the parents the "primary educators" of their children have any real meaning?

For Married Couples

How do you experience the exercise of your parental responsibilities as genuine co-parenting?
Are there any ways in which you do not experience co-parenting in your marriage?

What are the things you do that affirm a good self-image in your children?
Is there anything you do that may be an obstacle to their forming a good image of themselves?

Of the suggestions and guidelines offered in this chapter regarding the discipline of children, which three do you find closest to your own practice?
Which three are furthest away?

Do you experience that you are regarded as the primary educators of your children by the administrators and teachers in the school(s) your children attend? How or how not?

For Engaged Couples

What are the areas of agreement and of disagreement you have in regard to the notion of co-parenting?

Compare the way each of you experienced parental discipline when you were growing up. What are the major similarities and differences?

How do you think the manner in which each of you was brought up will affect your approach to the discipline of your children?

How compatible are the ideas each of you has regarding sex education of children?

How would you wish to approach the religious education of your own children?

Chapter 6

The Place of Work

If people want a ready made excuse for not investing in marital intimacy and family togetherness, it is right at hand: the career, the job. We all must work. We must make a living. So, without much difficulty we could easily allow the job to be all-consuming, if we choose.

The point, however, is that we don't have to choose to let the job control us. We can decide to put the job in its place—second to our marriage and our family.

In this chapter we examine the job inasmuch as it affects a marriage. How do we view our job? How do we set priorities and keep the job in the service of the marriage? Should both married partners have outside work? These are the kinds of questions that modern day couples must face at various times in their marital journey.

Attitudes

The first thing that couples have to do in regard to the job is to examine their attitudes toward it. Honestly addressing two questions will help reveal to the couple what their attitudes really are.

1. *In my mind is "the job" synonymous with "mean-*

ingful employment"? By "the job" here is meant an outside occupation for which a person receives financial remuneration. The term "meaningful employment" refers to occupations that have significance for one's own growth as a human being and for the well-being and enrichment of others.

The way a person answers this question influences one's attitude toward staying at home, taking care of children and managing the household. Ted believed that the only real employment was the paid job. "That's why men go out to work. Women can take care of the less important things." At social gatherings he always talked about his accomplishments, and often "teased" that he wasn't free, like his wife (who is the mother of four children), "to watch soap operas all day." Since he was "the breadwinner," he controlled the budget and decided what allotment his wife ought to have for household expenses. He was too busy with his career to "waste time" babysitting his children or helping with chores around the house. He even had recourse to religion to support his view. "God meant for man to do the world's work, and for women to do the housework. That's why God made them the way he did."

Barry's attitude was the opposite. While he realized money had to be brought into the house, he believed that the real value of work was what it was doing to people in human terms. He hated his job as a salesman, but dutifully did it during the years his wife Alice took care of their five children. Even during those years, he spent as much time with the children as he could. While Alice enjoyed being at home, she also missed her work as a commercial artist. When the youngest child was two, Barry and Alice switched roles. She went back to her art work and he became a house-husband. He enjoyed having more time with the children and having the opportunity to get to know them better.

In Ted's view employment was only meaningful if it was an outside paying job. Unfortunately, much of American society reflects his view. The government will pay for child-care service to allow mothers to go outside the house and work, but they will not pay them to stay home and take care of their children. Praise is given for people's accomplishments outside the home, but the creative energy expended in rearing children is largely ignored and taken for granted. In a discussion some years ago about tax deductions for dependent children, an unmarried person opposed such breaks in these words: "No one asked them to have children. That's their problem."

Barry's view is the more insightful. Not all paying jobs are meaningful employment. Not all meaningful employment pays. Barry is more concerned that he and Alice find employment that is the most meaningful to the both of them and to the children.

2. *Is being a successful person synonymous with success on the job?* Unfortunately, in our American culture success is usually measured by how much money a person makes and how high s/he climbs the promotional ladder. One is considered "successful" in business according to the amount of financial profits made. Whether one's business has made a contribution to human development and bettered the lives of the employees is a very secondary consideration. An author is regarded as "successful" if the book has sold a million copies. The book's literary and cultural worth enters far less into the picture. One's "success" as an executive depends on how close s/he has come to being the top administrator. What one has done for the well-being of people in the organization is overlooked.

Much of the American attitude toward success is summed up in two remarks that, in substance, are heard often enough. "He climbed all over his grandmother and anyone else who got in the way. But you've got to hand it to him, he made a success of himself and got to the top." "Poor Jack, he's a really nice guy, but he's just not tough enough to be successful in this 'dog-eat-dog' world."

Each married person must ask herself/himself whether or not s/he is going to buy into the value system dictated by the culture. Each must face the question: "What makes me a successful person—being a good spouse and parent, or having a high-paying job?" How we set up our priorities depends on the way we answer this question.

The Marriage First, The Job Second

Ann was satisfied with her situation. It was what she had agreed upon when she got married, and continued to accept after twenty-three years. "He told me when we first got serious that his business would always be his first love; I would always be his second love. I wanted him, so I was willing to take him on that condition."

Beatrice was less satisfied with her husband's priorities, but nonetheless resigned. "His first three loves are his job, his golf, and his wife—in that order. But what can I do?"

Charlene is of a different stripe. She would not tolerate second or third place in her husband's life. "When I went to the altar, I promised that I would have him as the number one love in my life. I expect the same of him. I want to be married to a man, not to his career."

If people are satisfied with their situation, who can argue? Our own personal view, however, is consonant with Charlene's. The relationship with one's spouse, and then with one's children, ought to have priority over one's job or career.

There are a few things that a couple can do to ensure that their jobs will serve the marriage, and not vice versa.

1. *Prior to the marriage they need to discuss their priorities and make sure they agree on them.* If there are differences, and one spouse thinks the career ought to come first and the other believes the marriage should, they either have to resolve that difference or decide that their priorities are incompatible.

2. *Decisions about working on a job much over forty hours a week ought to involve the input of both spouses.* Emily was very much upset with her husband Gerry. He was a dental technician who worked on a weekly salary basis for a group of dentists. He was paid for a 9-to-5 job. The work kept piling up. Gerry was a timid man, and the senior dentist was very aggressive. To keep up with the work Gerry started coming in at 7:30 and staying until 6 and then 6:30 in the evening, all for the same pay. When he started going in on Saturday, Emily forced a showdown.

Len was becoming increasingly irritated with his wife Gloria. She was a very conscientious English teacher at the local high school. She gave her five classes of thirty-five students each all sorts of quizzes, tests and composition assignments. "Every night she's correcting papers from after dinner until at least ten. And forget the weekends. It's papers, papers, papers. I've had it."

These two situations illustrate one way in which the job can dominate. People out of fear or sincere zeal can begin putting in fifty-, sixty- and seventy-hour weeks for forty-hour pay. Their spouses have every right to complain when this begins to happen. Another way of doing more than an average work week is to work overtime for extra pay or to engage in moonlighting. The couple may agree that this is advisable because of the extra money it provides or because of the opportunity it affords. On the other hand, a spouse might raise a very legitimate objection because other responsibilities are being neglected. Whatever arrangement is decided upon, both spouses ought to be mutually satisfied.

3. *If a job is being allowed to dominate the marriage, a couple ought to examine the reasons.* It could be because of money, or the hope of advancement, or just plain love of the work. If any of these are the reasons, the couple have to examine their priorities. Or the reason might be that one is—at least, unwittingly—trying to escape intimacy. If this is the case, then the couple need to look at their entire relationship, and, possibly with the help of counseling, address the deeper issues.

The Two-Job Family

Mike and Rose were deeply upset with each other. They had been happily married for twenty years. Mike was a successful stockbroker. Rose, who had graduated from college with a business degree, had stayed home for all of that time taking care of their seven children. Now that the oldest was in college and the youngest had started elementary school, Rose wanted to get a part-time job. Mike's mother had never worked outside the home, and his father had prided himself on the fact that he was the sole support of the family. Mike was now very threatened by the possibility that his role of "sole support" would be taken from him. Rose, on the other hand, felt that she had more than "paid her dues" as a housewife. While not wishing to abrogate that role, she felt she had as much right as her husband to have an opportunity to try her other considerable skills.

Frank's opposition to Kate working was rooted in a different reason. He worked in a factory and saw "how the men make passes at the women." He also knew of some affairs that were taking place. "There is no way I will let my wife be exposed to that." "Anyway," he justified, "woman's place is in the home." Kate was incensed: "For years I've had to allow him to be exposed to members of the opposite sex. Now he doesn't trust me enough to allow the same for me."

The stories of these two couples illustrate some of the tensions that continue to exist regarding the topic of two spouses working. In many families the problem has been solved because of sheer exigency. "There is no way we could make ends meet if we both didn't work." In other households, however, the conflict has not been resolved. Here are some of our own personal convictions that might help the ongoing discussion.

1. *Women have as much right to develop their various talents and to put them to good use in outside jobs as do men.* Gone are the days when it seemed acceptable to view women as inferior to men. Numerous women are better educated and more talented than many men. It is unfair to women to prevent them from exercising their right to work. It is unjust to deprive human society of the enormous gifts that women can bring to the work force.

2. *Men have as much responsibility to be husbands and fathers as women do to be wives and mothers.* This is something we stressed in our earlier chapter on co-parenting. We repeat it here because one of the most frequently heard arguments against married women having careers or professions is that "women's place is in the

home." The religious version of that is that "God called women to be wives and mothers, not firefighters, doctors, or bankers." Well, what about men? God didn't call them to be husbands and fathers? If men have a call to be something more than husbands and fathers, why can't women have a call to be more than wives and mothers? Why should women be required more than men to balance spousal and parental responsibilities with an outside job?

3. *Long before the marriage, talk with each other about your attitudes toward a two-job family.* Whether you are in favor or opposed, there is no problem as long as both of you agree. Any disagreement on this issue needs to be dealt with before the wedding bells ring. For, underneath the opposition to a two-job family may well be deeply felt convictions that are based on sexist stereotypes. If this is the case, the couple may be locked into an irreconcilable conflict.

4. *It is also good to have agreed upon some specific plans in regard to two jobs in your own marriage.* Clara and Marty agreed that they would both pursue their careers for the first four years of their marriage. After that, they would have children and Clara would stay home until the youngest went to school. Monica and Charles decided that they were both going to work throughout their marriage. When children came along, Monica would take a two-month leave of absence and then find a sitting service for the children. Nettie and Brian wanted to keep their options open. Whoever was making the more money would work outside the home. The other would take care of the children.

These are the kinds of general arrangements that are good to talk about ahead of time. Such discussion can prevent a lot of possible future conflicts. Indeed, circumstances and feelings might change as the marriage proceeds. If that happens, the couple can then go back to the drawing board in an honest and open manner.

5. *When both spouses work they ought to affirm and support each other and take an interest in each other's jobs.* Spousal competitiveness is rather pathetic. "I make more money than she ever will." "His job is a piece of cake. I'm the one who really has to work for a living." "I'll move up the ladder. She'll be stuck on the same rung forever."

6. *Both ought to be willing to make adjustments and sacrifices for the sake of the other's career.* For centuries it was the wife who was expected to follow her husband's career. Carol moved nine times in fifteen years as Ray worked his way up the corporate ladder. Evelyn's thirteen moves during her husband's twenty-year military career took her from coast to coast and to six foreign countries. "We would get acclimated to one culture, and get the children settled in school, and then it would be 'off we go.' " If wives had jobs of their own, the moves were even more traumatic. "I used to have to give up my job on very short notice," Angie commented. "After we would get settled, I would go searching for whatever I could find."

Now that more and more married women are entering professions and taking on careers of their own, there are two questions that every husband must ask himself. "Is it fair to expect my wife to give up or jeopardize her career for the sake of mine?" "How willing am I to move and to sacrifice my profession or career for the sake of my wife's job opportunity?" These are also the kinds of questions a couple would do well to discuss before they are married.

7. *If both are working outside the house both ought*

also to work inside the house. It is totally unacceptable that a wife with a full-time outside job is expected to do all the household tasks and child care while her husband "relaxes after a hard day." It is essential that husbands assume their fair share of these family responsibilities. Statistical studies show that this does not often happen.

8. *A special effort has to be made to spend sufficient time with each other and with the children.* It is possible that improving the quality of our time together can make up for the fact that we may have less time to spend with one another. However, it is a fallacy to think that less time is automatically going to mean better time. It takes energy, discipline and creativity to spend quality time together on a regular basis in the best of circumstances. When both partners are juggling two full-time jobs with all the other demands of family life, sheer exhaustion can become the biggest obstacle to intimate sharing.

Summary

In human terms, being meaningfully employed is more important than having "a successful job." If our priority is creating a mutually enriching marriage and building a closely knit family, then that will become our first employment. The outside job will take second place in our scale of values. Rather than sacrificing our marriage, our family, and ourselves on the altar of "worldly" achievement, we will measure success in terms of the humane qualities we have developed in ourselves and have helped nurture in our children. This priority will govern our approach to the job and to the related issue of two-job families.

Reflection Exercises

For All Readers

In order of importance, what, according to your view, are the essential ingredients for becoming a successful person?

How would you like to be remembered after you die?

For Married Couples

How has dedication to your job affected your marriage? Compare your answer to that of your spouse.

How do each of you feel about both spouses working outside the house?

Why do you feel this way?

For Engaged Couples

What is your view regarding which spouse should be "the breadwinner" in your marriage?

Why do you feel this way?

Compare your view with that of your fiancé(e).

Chapter 7

Money Matters

The college senior sat straight in his chair, looked across the office desk and seriously proclaimed: "My goal is to make my first million by the time I'm thirty. Then I'll worry about building relationships." Two remarks came immediately to mind. The first was: "Obviously, you do not intend to go into teaching." And the second: "Good luck!"

This student's conviction that money must come first, and his clear step-by-step explanation of how he was going to achieve his financial goals, were in stark contrast to a nineteen year old couple who had sat in the same office a few months earlier. They were "madly in love" and were going to get married the next month. At the end of her freshman year, Yvonne was going to quit college and take a job as a secretary until the baby came so that Mike could continue his three years of college. He would take night jobs to "bring in some bread" and to pay off their rather substantial college debts. "We're not worried. When you are in love, everything falls into place." "Maybe, but, pardoning the pun, don't bank on it."

Somewhere between these two opposite attitudes lies a balance. This chapter strives to explore the parameters of a reasonable approach to money matters in a marriage.

Ownership

Vivian and Don had ongoing fights over money. Don had a job that paid well. Vivian stayed home caring for their three children. Don was of the deep conviction that his salary was *his* hard-earned money. "I am the one who made it. I am the one who owns it." Surely he had financial responsibilities to his wife and children. These he "fulfilled" by allotting Vivian so much each week for food, clothing and other household essentials. Occasionally he would "throw in a little extra allowance" for his wife. Vivian complained that Don treated her like a child. "He never allows enough for me to make ends meet. Then he chides me for going over my allotment."

Don's behavior is rooted in a definite philosophical viewpoint regarding ownership in a marriage. According to this perspective, the salary you make is yours.

Our strongly held opinion is that what either spouse earns through an outside job belongs to both. "It is *our* money, for we are a partnership." Together the couple make decisions how their money is budgeted and managed. This joint ownership pertains, we believe, whether only one spouse has a salaried job, or both do.

In the past a few students have raised objections to this position. "What if he is addicted to gambling or is an alcoholic? What if she is an irresponsible spender who runs up huge debts? Do you mean to say that these kinds of spouses should be able to exercise co-ownership of the responsible spouse's money?" No we don't. Our answer to these objections is simply stated: If you are married to a financially irresponsible spouse, sew up your pocketbook. Then try to search for the appropriate therapy and counseling. But these are the exceptions. They do not deny the general principle.

Managing the Money

Hazel lived under the old stereotype. "When my husband was alive, he took care of all money matters. He designed the budget, wrote all the checks, paid the bills, and balanced the books. I never even knew what his salary was. But all the time I didn't mind. I just thought that was the way things were supposed to be. Now when I look back, I think it was a mistake. When my husband died, I didn't know anything about handling finances."

Bert and Rose took an opposite approach. Bert is an art teacher. His worst subject in school was arithmetic. "To this day I hate math. Balancing the checkbooks and figuring out taxes drive me crazy." Rose, on the other hand, has always been at ease managing money. After high school she lived on her own for five years, handling her own finances. During that time she also worked as a cashier in a large department store. They are both very happy with the arrangement they agreed upon long ago: Rose takes care of all the finances; Bert takes charge of the interior decorating.

The process whereby money is managed in the home is far more important than who actually does the book work. Here are some suggestions:

1. *Together the couple ought to agree on the assignment of financial tasks.* The decision should not be based on the sexist stereotype that in the past automatically assigned this job to the male. Interest, talent and time need

to be the determining factors. In some marriages one person may handle all the financial tasks on an indefinite basis. In other marriages spouses might either divide the tasks or take turns every other month or year. Whatever the arrangement, the essential thing is that both spouses be happy with it.

2. *Regardless of which spouse actually handles the finances, both ought to be able to do so.* If one has never had the experience, that one ought to learn and practice under the other's guidance.

3. *The spouse who keeps the books ought to keep the other spouse continually informed regarding what is going on with their finances.* Both spouses should also understand "the method of bookkeeping" being followed. This is especially true if it is a homemade method!

Financial Priorities

The most basic priority to be set is: Where does money fit into the marriage? Is marital intimacy our first priority, or is money? Let us assume that a couple agree that they both value their personal relationship as the foremost priority. Beyond that, they must set up a number of financial priorities. Some of this needs to be done at the beginning of the marriage. Many times during the marriage financial priorities change and need to be adjusted.

Cindy and Tom decided that they were going to have their family early rather than wait until they were "financially well off." Hence, they bought a modest house in a moderate income area. They decided they could get along with a second-hand car. The VCR and the computer would wait a long time.

Isabel and Dan had different ideas. They were both

from lower income families, and had worked their way through college. They were determined that they were going to give their children all of the things of which they had been deprived. Accordingly, they would postpone having children until they had made enough money to buy a large house in "a nice neighborhood" and have it well furnished with all the extras.

Whatever anyone wants to say about these two very different sets of priorities, the important point is that in each case the couple was in agreement. A *real* problem would arise if someone like Tom were married to someone like Isabel. That is why it is so important that some general financial priorities be agreed upon prior to marriage.

Even when both partners are operating out of the same basic set of priorities, specific priorities need to be discussed throughout the marriage. Are we going to get a new roof this year, or will we send Lisa to the orthodontist? Will we take a vacation this summer, or are we going to put the money into a fancier car? Do we replace the worn-out carpet, or do we have the outside of the house repainted? Setting these kinds of priorities demands mature, free dialogue and the mutual agreement of both spouses.

Living Within One's Means

Ann and Vin sat down three weeks before they got married and planned a careful budget. They owed $8,000 for their college education and decided they would pay that off before they incurred any other debts. They allowed so much a month for rent, food, clothing, transportation, entertainment, and other sundries. They also put a certain amount of money into two savings accounts: one for short-range goals such as additional furniture and a dishwasher, and one for the longer-range goal of buying a house. They scrupulously kept within their overall budget, though they would sometimes spend more on one item, such as food, and less on another, as, for example, clothing. Periodically in their marriage, as income changed, prices rose, and children came along, they would revise their budget. But their principle was always the same. "We do not spend what we don't have." They also always put something away "for the unknown future," even if it was only a few dollars from each paycheck.

Virginia and Andy followed the same basic principle, namely, spend only what you have in hand. However, they did not like to be tied down to a formal budget. "We know what we make each month. We also know the general range of certain basic expenses like housing, insurance premiums, gas, electricity and water. The rest we spend until it runs out, and then wait for the next check. We just make sure that our money doesn't run out too early in the month."

Many couples find that in the beginning of the marriage it is good to start with a very structured budget as did Ann and Vin. After a year or two they find themselves adopting the approach of Virginia and Andy. Whichever approach a couple is more comfortable with is fine. The important thing is to stay within one's means. As a very close friend of ours once put it, "Don't live a champagne life on a soft drink budget!"

Bernice and Tim now wish they had heard that advice. Instead, they were taken in by the unconscionable campaign launched by savings and loan companies that urge us to "live now and pay later." They were hoodwinked by the continued barrage of advertising that would have us confuse our wants with our needs.

When they got married, Bernice and Tim already owed a substantial amount for their college education. They both got good jobs after graduation, but did not realize how easily even fairly decent salaries can be absorbed by debt. They bought a house and two cars on loan. They also ran up their credit card bills for home appliances, furniture and clothing. "With the kind of jobs we have we must be in style." After the "ninety days without payment" had quickly sped by, Bernice and Tim realized that they could hardly make ends meet. Tim's motorcycle accident that necessitated several knee surgeries and Bernice's unexpected pregnancy complicated the financial picture and drove them near to panic. Many arguments and much fighting ensued. It took both financial counseling and marriage therapy to help Bernice and Tim to straighten out their money problems and salvage their marriage.

Money, it is said, is one of the major topics about which couples argue. A great deal of those arguments, we believe, can be avoided if couples budget properly and agree to live within their means. In this way they will forestall many of the tensions that come with overspending and being in debt. Let us summarize here some practical guidelines that can help a couple live within their means and avoid possible marital problems due to finances.

1. Together line up your short-range and long-range financial goals that are possible within the framework of your expected income.

2. Draw up a monthly budget. Leave some cushion for unexpected expenses. Do not make major expenditures without mutual agreement. (The couple ought to agree on what they mean by major expenditures.) You might, however, want to allow each other a certain

amount of unaccountable money, what we like to call "mad money."

3. For the most part, do not buy what you cannot presently afford. Don't abuse credit cards. While they are good for emergencies, and for establishing credit, they can also be one's financial downfall. Be very reluctant to carry more than one or two major debts at a time. That's about all the person of average income can comfortably handle.

4. If at all possible take some of your monthly salary (even if it is only a few dollars) and put it into savings. This gives you something to fall back on in the uncertain future.

5. Together, distinguish your wants from your true needs. Needs must take priority over wants. Saving something for tomorrow's needs may have to take priority over satisfying all immediate wants.

6. Discern which kind of checking and savings accounts are best for the two of you: separate or joint where only one signature is required, joint where both signatures are necessary. We have heard financial experts give opposite advice in regard to separate or joint accounts. In light of the lack of agreement on the part of the experts, we chose joint accounts that require the signature of either one of us. For us, this speaks of our mutual trust in each other's responsibility and fidelity. This approach, however, is inadvisable if one has reason to doubt a spouse's sense of financial responsibility.

If you do have joint checking accounts have a simple way to keep each other informed of your balance. One couple we know do this by registering a certain percentage of every deposit in the wife's checkbook and the remaining percentage in the husband's checkbook. The percentage depends on the number of bills each is going to take care of in the given month. Neither spouse exceeds the amount in her/his checkbook without first consulting the other.

A Christian Approach to Money

A couple who wish to share their Christian faith and live their married life in light of Gospel values do well to examine their attitudes toward money and their use of money in light of Christian insights. Four of these insights can be reviewed here.

1. In the Scriptures God is the Creator of all reality. Hence, he is the ultimate owner. As William Byron points out in his small but poignant book, *Toward Stewardship,* we creatures are stewards of the earth for the relatively short period we are here. We are, then, accountable to God for the way we use material things. We came to life on this earth owning no *thing,* and we make our final exit leaving every *thing* behind. What we bring to the other side of the grave is *who* we have become as loving human beings.

Married couples can ask themselves to what degree they live out this attitude in their marriage. Do we hoard material things or use them to serve others? Do we waste resources, letting the water run endlessly, keeping lights on when they are not being used, or allowing the house to get unnecessarily warm in the winter and cool in the summer? Are we in control of things or have we permitted them to rule us?

2. The Gospels emphasize the value of the *spirit* of poverty. The virtue of poverty spoken of in the New Testament is not to be confused with destitution. In fact, the Christian is commanded by Christ to fight destitution and to minister to the needs of the deprived.

Nor is the evangelical virtue of poverty rooted in a pessimistic view of physical reality. The preaching of Jesus reflects a very sensitive appreciation of the beauties of nature and the goodness of things. The Gospel testimony makes clear that Jesus did not follow the ascetical practices of John the Baptist.

What the Gospel virtue of poverty is all about is setting persons as a priority over things. People are more important than material things. Hence, persons ought not to be sacrificed for the sake of accumulating wealth. Money must be sacrificed for the sake of people.

Do a couple agree on this value system in their marriage? Do they both believe that the gift of personal presence to one another and to their children is of much greater value than material things? Do they spend their money on activities that can bind the family closer together rather than on keeping up with "the latest styles"?

3. Trust in God's providence is another important virtue that is underscored in the Gospel. There are two extremes that people can fall into in this regard. On the one hand, some think that they must do it all by themselves, as if they were left entirely to their own ingenuity. Overwork and anxiety result. In the other extreme are those who think that God provides magically without the cooperation of humans. "We will wait for a miracle."

The New Testament makes clear the need for humans to cooperate with God. Such cooperation avoids both of the above extremes. In the Gospel Jesus tells a parable, followed by a lesson that points to a balanced approach:

> There was once a rich man who, having had a good harvest from his land, thought to himself, "What am I to do? I have not enough room to store my crops." Then he said, "This is what I will do: I will pull down my barns and build bigger

ones, and store all my grain and my goods in them, and I will say to my soul: My soul, you have plenty of good things laid by for many years to come; take things easy, eat, drink, have a good time." But God said to him, "Fool! This very night the demand will be made for your soul; and this hoard of yours, whose will it be then?" So it is when a man stores up treasure for himself in place of making himself rich in the sight of God (Lk 12:16–21).

Then he said to his disciples, "That is why I am telling you not to worry about your life and what you are to eat, nor about your body and how you are to clothe it. For life means more than food, and the body more than clothing. Think of the ravens. They do not sow or reap; they have no storehouses and no barns; yet God feeds them. And how much more are you worth than the birds! Can any of you, for all his worrying, add a single cubit to his span of life? If the smallest things, therefore, are outside your control, why worry about the rest? Think of the flowers; they never have to spin or weave; yet I assure you, not even Solomon in all his regalia was robed like one of these. Now if that is how God clothes the grass in the field which is there today and thrown into the furnace tomorrow, how much more will he look after you, you men of little faith! But you, you must not set your hearts on things to eat and things to drink; nor must you worry. It is the pagans of this world who set their hearts on all these things. Your Father well knows you need them. No; set your hearts on his kingdom, and these other things will be given you as well" (Lk 12:22–31).

Christian couples do well to ask themselves whether or not they really believe this. If we do indeed believe these insights, how do we put them into practice in our marriage?

4. Finally, another essential aspect of a Christian approach to money is generosity toward the needy. A recurring theme in the prophetic literature of the Old Testament is almsgiving. The prophets insisted that an integral part of true religion was caring for the poor and the deprived, especially the widow and the orphan. In his preaching Jesus specified that entrance into the kingdom of heaven depends on how we have fed the hungry, clothed the naked, given drink to the thirsty, and visited the sick and the imprisoned.

A married couple need to avoid turning in on themselves and their family. While it is true that our primary responsibility lies within the home, the family does not exist merely for itself. It is meant to reach out and enrich the wider human community, and to share with those who are less fortunate. Often this giving will come from our abundance. Sometimes it should also come from our lack of abundance. By reaching out to others the family avoids becoming self-centered. Family members become more aware of the human condition, as well as more sensitive and compassionate. These are virtues that enable the family to become a more closely knit unit.

There are several ways in which a family can share its material resources. The first obvious one is by giving money. We are all so barraged by appeals for money that the temptation can be to turn a deaf ear entirely. Churches, research centers, alma maters, political parties, lobbying groups, Girl/Boy Scouts, hospitals and charitable societies are just some of the organizations competing for our funds. A couple ought to discuss together how much money they are able and willing to give to others. Then they need to agree on a priority list of those organizations that will receive their gifts.

One couple we know follow a very careful set of guidelines. They give to organizations with the least amount of overhead, and to those groups who work most directly with the poor and needy. "We refused to give to the parish appeal for remodeling the Church with more comfortable pews and air conditioning. We wrote our check instead to the parish St. Vincent de Paul Society." Another couple have boycotted the Peter's Pence collection. "We don't believe in supporting that bureaucracy over there." Instead they send a periodic check to the medical missionaries. Whatever way they decide, the important thing is that a couple give what they can, and see that their money goes for causes that they believe will benefit their fellow humans the most.

There are, of course, other ways to give besides through direct financial contributions. In some families those members who are eligible become regular blood donors at a community blood center. Others go through the inconvenience of saving old papers and magazines for the next paper drive. Still others save old clothes, toys and books. Instead of having a garage sale they send them to charitable organizations. Many couples donate their time as volunteers in any number of charitable activities.

Much more could be said about a Christian approach to money. The four points developed in this section are essential components to such an approach. They can serve, at least, as a starting point for a couple's efforts to apply Gospel values to the financial area of their marriage.

Summary

Money in itself is neither the savior nor the demon that some make it out to be. It will not magically bring happiness. Nor will it necessarily bring destruction. Its value or non-value comes from our attitudes and our decisions. The proper use of money allows people to develop their talents, to achieve a human level of living, to enrich meaningful relationships, and to serve their fellow humans. On the other hand, if people permit money to own them, it can rob them of their humanness and destroy the possibility of human communion.

No couple can ignore the meaning that money has in their marriage. The challenge is to put money in the employ of the marriage, rather than sacrifice growth in intimacy for the sake of money.

Reflection Exercises

For All Readers

What are the important values that money can add to a marriage?
What are the pitfalls in regard to money that a couple need to avoid?
What strengths of character and what weaknesses of character can make the difference between whether money will benefit or hinder the marital relationship?

For Married Couples

What main arguments in your marriage have you had in regard to money?
How did you resolve these arguments?
What are your present financial goals?
How do they compare to those of your spouse?
In what ways have you allowed Gospel values to govern your use of money in your marriage?
In what ways have you not done so?

For Engaged Couples

Are your views concerning ownership in a marriage compatible?
Who in your marriage will handle the finances?
List your financial priorities for the first two years of your marriage. Compare your list with that of your fiancé(e).

Chapter 8

Old and New Relationships

On the wedding day, the marriage is not the only new relationship that comes into being. We enter into a new kind of relationship with our parents, our siblings, and our friends. We are now the married daughter, the married son, the married friend. Old forms of relating must give way to different ones.

Also on the wedding day we become bonded to a new family. We take on a special relationship to our spouse's parents, relatives and friends.

All of these changes present us with a challenge that calls for many adjustments. It is to these changed relationships and to the adjustments they demand that we now turn.

Families, Old and New

Perhaps the biggest obstacle for married people getting along with their parents and in-laws is the persistent belief that it is not possible. In-laws are just not supposed to be able to like each other. Comedians' jokes and certain advertising skits that poke fun especially at mothers-in-law reinforce the stereotype.

The basic premise for the guidelines given here is that, while there can be difficulties that need to be worked through, it is to be expected that most of us will be able to find new and mature ways of relating to our parents, and that we will discover new friendships with our in-laws.

1. *Be sensitive to the new situation that your marriage has created not only for yourself but also for your parents.* Everyone is aware of the dramatic change that has taken place in the lives of the couple on the wedding day. Often we forget that a parallel change, perhaps as dramatic, has also taken place in the lives of the couple's parents.

Ordinarily the parents have lived under the same roof with their sons and daughters for at least eighteen years. The parents were the nurturers and guardians. Intimate bonds have been established. After the wedding most of that is changed. There is physical separation—sometimes by hundreds of miles. The parents no longer have a nurturing and guardian role. They must let go. While the intimate bonding will hopefully ever remain and grow, there is no longer the opportunity of the day-to-day companionship and communication.

Newlyweds need to be aware of the pain both sets of parents may be going through. They also have to be aware of the need and desire their parents have for ongoing contact. While not allowing undue parental interference, the couple ought to see that they both keep the friendship going with their parents. Letters, phone calls, visits, and occasionally meeting one's parents for lunch or dinner ought to become an integral part of the marriage. Each spouse needs to encourage the other to keep up this kind of contact.

Many problems can ensue when this kind of reasonable contact is cut off or blocked. Greg is an example. He had never really outgrown his adolescent rebellion against parental figures. When he got married he insisted on moving to a distant city. He announced to his parents that he was embarking on a new life now and did not want their interference. He discouraged visits and phone calls, and wrote only rarely. This caused a great deal of hard feeling, not only with his parents, but also with his wife Stephanie. She actually liked her in-laws, and thought Greg was being unreasonable. Matters got much worse when Greg started seriously curtailing Stephanie's contact with her own family. He forbade visits and clocked her phone calls. Many fights ensued. Stephanie finally announced that she would not take this kind of behavior anymore.

2. *Be willing to dialogue with your parents.* Wisdom does not automatically come with age. Nor does it automatically disappear. "Your ideas are no longer relevant to today's world," the fifteen year old solemnly announced to her thirty-eight year old mother not long ago. "No offense, but at your age people are out of touch."

Most of our parents have achieved wisdom that can come with experience and age. They have been married a long time, reared children, and have learned from the ups and downs that come with life. So we can listen to their advice, give it due consideration, and then make our own decision. Where the advice seems reasonable, we can learn. When we disagree, we can do so with sensitivity, and without giving unnecessary offense.

3. *Try to become friends with your in-laws.* The starting point for entering into relationship with our in-laws ought not to be all the possible problems we have heard about so much. Rather the starting point should be what we have going for us.

What spouses have going for them are two significant realities. The first is the fact that they are in love with one another. The second is the fact that one's in-laws are people who are near and dear to one's spouse. When we love another person, the people whom that person loves take on special meaning for us. If we enter into our spouse's feelings for her/his parents and siblings, this will enable us to take a positive approach in relating to them.

4. *The parental relationship must yield to the primacy of the marital relationship.* The marriage comes first. Responsibilities to parents, serious though they be, come second. When there is a conflict of interests, the couple should support each other in upholding the marriage as their foremost priority. They cannot allow parents or anyone else to split their undivided loyalty.

When John, an only child, was nineteen, his father died suddenly. John's mother never really reconciled herself to her husband's death. Three and a half years after his death, she still kept his study the way he had left it when he had died. Not even his ashtray was emptied.

John became his mother's crutch. At her insistence he left the university he had been attending in another state, returned home and enrolled in a small local college. His mother manipulated him into doing all sorts of chores and spending most of his free time with her. John allowed his mother to put him on all sorts of guilt trips.

After John was engaged to Bea, his mother became quite jealous. Whenever they had made a date, his mother would suddenly need him at home. The increasing number of broken dates began to disturb Bea. The final blow came when his mother vetoed most of the wedding plans that Bea and John had agreed upon. John backed down and sided with his mother. Bea gave John an ultimatum: "Choose me or your mother." John chose his mother. Bea was wise to realize that if his mother could control John that much during the engagement period, she would continue to control him after the marriage.

Linda and Frank handled a similar kind of situation in a very different way. Linda's parents were very domineering and over-protective of her. They did not approve of Frank. This didn't bother Linda too much, because her parents had never approved of any boy friend she had brought home. After graduating from college Linda moved out of the house, and, much to the chagrin of her parents, got an apartment of her own. Much as Linda loved her parents, she determined early in the relationship that she and Frank must make the major decisions that affect their lives, and stand united before her parents. Predictably, her parents opposed the January date they had set for the wedding. "Wait till June." They also opposed the simplicity of the wedding reception that Linda and Frank chose. "It should be in a hotel, not the parish hall." Linda and Frank prevailed. They also prevailed in their decision to settle in a city a hundred and fifty miles away from Linda's parents. After a couple of years Linda's parents have finally come to accept Frank and the independence that he and Linda chose for themselves.

5. *You are your children's parents; your parents are the grandparents.* There is a delicate balance to be maintained here. How, on the one hand, do we assume our rights and responsibilities as parents and protect ourselves from undue interference, and yet, on the other hand, allow our parents the rights and responsibilities that belong to grandparenting?

"From the day we returned from the honeymoon," Grace complained, "my parents have been bugging me about when Al and I were going to make them grandparents. I am absolutely tired of it. It is none of their business!"

"I have ambivalent feelings about my parents visiting here," Bridget mused. "I love to see them, and they are great with our four children. But I get so sick of being told that I don't dress them warmly enough, that their diet isn't perfect, that I'm not consistent in the way I discipline them. Sometimes I could scream."

Recently, however, two grandparents expressed another perspective. "Our son and his wife act as if they own their two children. When they are around, they don't want us to do anything for their children. They won't accept any of our advice, even though we reared eight children of our own. Yet, when they want to go out and need a free babysitter, we are the ones they always call. They can't have it both ways."

These three sets of comments illustrate the kinds of tensions that can exist in the parent-grandparent relationship. Grandparents—and potential ones—must respect the rights of their children to decide if and when they are going to become parents, how many children they are going to have, and how they are going to rear their own children. Advice is appropriate. Interference is not. Sometimes it might take a Solomon to determine where appropriate advice has crossed over into inappropriate interference.

At the same time parents need to acknowledge the wonderful gift of grandparenting. The authors regret that their own children have only known their maternal grandmother. Their other three grandparents had died long before they were born. Wonderful as their relationship with the one grandparent is, it does not make up for the loss of the other three.

Couples need to cherish the beautiful relationships that can develop between their children and the grandparents. Such relationships are important and enriching for all concerned. An atmosphere ought to be created that fosters the growth of these relationships. Without abandoning their prerogative as parents, couples need to give sufficient room for their own parents to be grandparents, and for their own children to be grandchildren. Allow them time to be together. Be flexible. Some "spoiling" on the part of grandparents can be permitted. Rejoice in the unique bonding that can develop. It is sometimes very special. And, alas, the opportunity goes by far too quickly!

6. *Respect the problem areas that may exist between your spouse and her/his parents or siblings.* So far we have been addressing the topic of in-laws under the general assumption that a basically good relationship exists between the couple and their parents. Obviously this is not always the case. If one's fiancé(e) or spouse "hates" one of her/his parents or siblings, special problems are in store. We have also been assuming that a person would have only one set of in-laws with whom to deal. That is getting to be less and less the case. Blended families complicate the picture. Some reflections on each of these situations are in order.

If one's spouse does not get along with one or more of her/his immediate relatives, this necessarily puts an added strain on relating to one's in-laws. In such a situation there are several cautions to keep in mind. These can be illustrated in the story of Jan and Will.

Jan wants nothing to do with her father. He has been an alcoholic for as long as she can remember. She resents deeply all of the physical and verbal abuse he heaped on her mother and on the children. While she loves her mother, Jan thinks she should have divorced her father years ago. In the six months she has been married to Will, she has refused to visit home when the father is there, even though she lives only a half hour away. She does get together with her mother and her three brothers and sisters as often as possible, whenever her father is not around.

There are several ways in which Will can best handle this situation. First, respect and understand Jan's feelings and the reasons for them. Do a lot of listening, both to Jan's words as well as her tears, her anger and her pain.

Second, Will ought to avoid the temptation to be judgmental or to play messiah: "It is wrong to be so angry at your father." "You should try to get along with him." "You're only running away from the problem." "He's really a nice man when he's not drinking." Pronouncements such as these come across as lacking empathy. They do no good, and only block further communication. Will does much better to allow Jan to talk out her feelings and to work through her problem. Through careful dialogue that includes feedback and sensitively posed questions, he can facilitate Jan's working through her feelings and drawing her own conclusions. Within that context he can contribute some guidance and much support.

Third, Will ought not make end runs around Jan; that is, he needs to avoid making contact with Jan's father on his own. "I got together with your father for lunch today. We had a really nice time. I don't know what your problem is." Any contact Will initiates with Jan's father should only result from dialogue with Jan and take place with their mutual agreement.

Finally, Will ought to avoid initiating criticism of Jan's father. Somehow, blood is still thicker than water. It's one thing for Jan to call her father "a drunken bum." If Will were to refer to Jan's father the same way, he might find Jan getting quite defensive. Will does well to support Jan in her conflict with her father. However, he ought not to let himself get caught in the middle of the fray. If he does, he may get it from both sides.

The other factor that can complicate relating to one's in-laws is the blended family. The chances are dramatically increasing that one's spouse is from a family where divorce has struck at least once.

One day in class some years ago, when the topic of in-laws was being discussed, a recently married student in her twenties frankly shared her family background. "My father and mother were divorced when I was five. He since has been remarried three times; my mother has been remarried twice. I have four half-brothers and sisters from three of those remarriages. I don't get along too well with my parents' present spouses, but I remain very close to my father's third wife and my mother's second husband."

All of this is just to say that the in-law issue today can get very complicated. One might need a chart or a road map. The best advice in these kinds of situations is to follow your spouse's lead in working your way through the complexities of blended and reblended in-law families.

Friends, Old and New

Each spouse also brings into the marriage a body of present and past friendships. Three sets of questions emerge. How as a married person do I now relate to my friends? How do I respond to my spouse's friends? How do we establish separate and joint friendships in the future? Perhaps the best way to address these interrelated issues is through a series of suggestions.

1. We need to acknowledge the fact that it is valuable and necessary for both spouses to have friendships be-

yond the marriage. No couple can satisfy all of each other's needs and interests. We have to have other people with whom to talk and to share.

Such friendships not only enrich the couple, but they also help prevent the couple from getting too closed in on one another. Rather than making the couple introverted, authentic intimacy strengthens them to reach out to other people and to form relationships with a wider circle of friends.

Accordingly, couples ought to encourage each other to keep up their friendships and to cultivate new friends. They ought to respect these relationships and afford each other sufficient time and space to maintain them.

2. While marriage ought not to put an end to old friendships, it does, however, transform them. The newlywed is no longer merely "one of the girls" or "one of the boys" but a married person. Hence, s/he should relate to her/his friends accordingly.

When Liz and Milt came for counseling, their eight month old marriage was in serious trouble. They both had gone to work after high school, and got married when they were twenty. Milt continued to hang around with the group he was close to in high school. He spent three or four nights a week with them and one day on the weekend, bowling, playing golf, basketball, and cards, and drinking. "He'll be out to all hours, come home half tanked, and then wake me up and want to have sex," Liz complained.

Milt clearly had not grown out of his bachelor days. He had failed to make the proper social adjustments appropriate for marriage. His male cronies were for companionship, his wife for sex.

Friendships have a place in marriage. But they need to be secondary to the marital relationship. One's spouse ought to be one's best friend.

3. Wives need to have as much opportunity to spend time with their friends as do their husbands. One husband insisted that he have one day off a week to fish, hunt, or golf with his friends, and one evening a week to spend with them. On the other hand, he strongly opposed his wife going out with her friends. "Her place is to be with the children when I'm gone, and with me when I'm home." This is just another example of how sexist inequity has crept into some marriages. Sensitive husbands will make sure that their wives have the same opportunity to establish and maintain friendships beyond the household as they do. Special effort in this regard will have to be made if the wife does not work outside the home and spends her days and nights taking care of small children.

There is another way in which inequity can manifest itself in regard to friends. The husband has his friends to the house, but is very intolerant of his wife having her friends over. One wife noted: "It's all right for his friends to come and smoke the place out. I'm expected to serve them refreshments. When my friends come for an evening, he calls it 'cackling ladies night,' and takes off." Another wife commented: "My husband likes us to throw two big parties a year, one on Super Bowl day and one on Kentucky Derby day. They are all his friends who come over. I do all the work."

4. Married couples need also to have mutual friends. This can happen in two ways. First, as the spouses together socialize with others, they will develop new friends who will relate to them as a married couple. Second, in a good marriage, individual friendships will be shared. Spouses will talk to one another about their friends and will meet and get to know many of one another's friends. Your friends take on meaning for me, because they are people who have meaning for you.

5. Friendships with members of the opposite sex continue to have a place in marriage. One of the marks of a mature, sexually developed person is the ability to relate meaningfully to persons who belong to the opposite gender. Marriage should actually improve one's ability in this regard. It should help the couple relate more comfortably with the other half of the human race. In a good marriage a couple can put aside undue fears and irrational jealousies and can support each other in achieving a balance in relating to others.

At the same time obvious cautions are called for in such relationships. The first key is honesty with oneself. Is this merely a friendship or are we getting emotionally involved? The second key is honesty with one's spouse. Is a person sharing this friendship with her/his spouse, or is an air of secretiveness entering the picture?

Summary

The end of the second creation account in the Book of Genesis pictures it well: "... a man leaves his father and mother and joins himself to his wife, and they become one body" (Gen 2:24). The primacy of the marital relationship comes through in this biblical passage. All other relationships—those with one's family of birth, one's in-laws and one's friends—are subordinate to the marital relationship. Yet, marriage does not insulate us from other people. Authentic marital intimacy enables us to grow in mature relationship with our relatives and friends. It empowers us to expand our horizons and to reach out and welcome new friends into the ambit of our life.

Reflection Exercises

For All Readers

What are some of the common misconceptions about in-laws that can block the building of good relationships with them?

Give your own personal opinion of this statement: "One's spouse ought to be one's best friend."

What place do you see in a marriage for friendships with members of the opposite sex?

Describe the concrete differences between being a friend with a person of the opposite sex, and being in love; between going to lunch with this person, and engaging in a luncheon date.

For Married Couples

How have each of you gotten along with your in-laws?

What are the things you like best in the way you and your in-laws relate?

What are the difficulties you experience?

How can these difficulties be resolved?

Were there ever any conflict situations in which you were forced to choose between your spouse and your blood relatives?

How did you address those conflict situations?

For Engaged Couples

How well have you gotten to know your fiancé(e)'s parents and siblings?

- Have you experienced any difficulties so far in relating to your future in-laws?
- Do you see any potential problems in relating to your parents and your in-laws that could develop after you are married? If so, how do you and your fiancé(e) plan to address these problems?

Chapter 9

Marriage with a Difference

Obviously, every marriage is between two persons who are different: different in gender, in physical makeup, in temperament, in tastes, and in interests. If there is a strong bond of commonality, these differences can make for excitement in the marriage and have a balancing and complementing effect on the spouses. If the bond is not strong, differences can be allowed to stand in the way of growing intimacy. They can block communication and can gnaw at the marital relationship.

The preceding chapters have touched on a number of differences that can exist between a couple. In this chapter we wish to concentrate on the more extraordinarily marked differences that can be present in some marriages in any one of three areas: religion, race, and age. Admittedly, extraordinary differences can also exist in other areas, such as social class and education. We limit ourselves to the three we have chosen, because they are each becoming more common today. Hence, these differences demand special consideration. Among the questions to be asked are these: What are the particular problems that a notable difference can pose for our own relationship, for our families, and for our children? How, on a realistic and practical level, are we going to address these problems?

Anyone who says that "love will take care of it all" is engaging in self-delusion and is paving the way for future storms. Honest soul-searching, frank dialogue and careful planning before the marriage are the best way to integrate the differences into a happy marriage and a sound future.

Religious Differences

As everyone who is minimally versed in history knows, differences in religious belief and practice have been allowed to destroy many human relationships. In the name of preserving the "true religion," humans have waged "holy wars" and have burned "heretics" at the stake. Churches have split and split again over such issues as the extent of the Pope's authority, marriage of the clergy, the date of Easter, and whether organ music can be played at worship services. Are we then surprised that religious differences—serious ones as well as not so serious ones—can pose a hazard to building a happy marriage?

In the past, when treating religious differences in marriage, we tended to be too narrow in our concerns. We concentrated exclusively on the faith differences that existed between spouses of different religions or denominations, and ignored the profound religious differences that can be present in marriages of persons of the same denomination.

We also lacked precision in our terminology. We called marriages between persons of different religions or denominations "mixed." The difficulty with this word is that it is too general. Actually every marriage is mixed (in gender, in individuality, and in personality and character traits). The term also applies to the dramatic mix in an interracial marriage and in "May-December" marriages.

The terminology was improved after the Second Vatican Council. We began speaking of marriages between people of different religions or denominations as "interfaith" marriages. The use of this term, however, is also problematic. First of all, it makes no distinction between marriages of people who belong to different religions, and marriages of people who are affiliated with diverse denominations of the same religion. Second, it fails to recognize that every marriage, even one between persons of the same denomination, has an interfaith dimension that ought not be ignored.

We, then, prefer to speak of *three* kinds of interfaith marriages: interreligional, interdenominational, and intradenominational. Let us consider the issues involved in each of these three types of interfaith marriages.

Interreligion Marriages

By "interreligion marriages" we mean marriages between two people who belong to different world religions. Examples would be marriages between a Jew and a Christian, or a Moslem and a Christian. These types of marriages need to be given a different kind of attention than interdenominational marriages for two reasons. First, they involve far more basic faith differences than interdenominational marriages. The principal difference between Christians and the other world religions centers around belief in Jesus. Traditional Christian belief proclaims Jesus as the Son of God, the Word of God enfleshed, and as Savior of all humanity. While the religion of Islam and many Jews consider Jesus a prophet, they cannot accept the Christian claim that he is God's Son. Second, marriages between Christians and Jews or Moslems involve greater cultural differences than most interdenominational marriages do, since these religions are very much linked to ethnic groups.

Judith was from a committed, conservative Jewish family. Ambrose was a Baptist. They met in graduate school and discovered they had a great deal in common. They dated for four months before they ever brought up the topic of their diverse religions. Even then, they only spoke of it superficially. "It's no big deal," Ambrose stated. While he was somewhat involved with his own Baptist tradition, he was also willing to attend the synagogue occasionally. "After all," he observed, "Christianity comes out of the Jewish religion."

Shortly after they were engaged, Judith became more concerned with the issue. She had two non-negotiable positions. First, she could not worship in a Christian church. "Jesus was a Jewish prophet, and a good man, but cannot be worshiped as Christians do." Second, any children of the marriage would have to be brought up in the Jewish religion. Ambrose had no difficulty accepting Judith's refusal to participate in Christian worship. He could not, however, accept her second condition. "No child of mine can be brought up Jewish." Many long and tearful discussions revealed that Judith and Ambrose had reached an impasse on a matter that was very important to each of them. They decided that in fairness to one another they must break off the engagement.

The situation of Martha and Abdul took a different turn. Martha was Episcopalian, but from high school days she had taken a great interest in the study of world religions. While deeply committed to her Christian faith, she always held the Islamic religion in high esteem.

Throughout their dating and their engagement period they discussed religion a great deal. While Abdul did not accept the divinity of Jesus, he considered him one of the greatest of the prophets. They were both comfortable allowing each other to worship in their separate places. Abdul felt that, as mother, Martha should be responsible for raising any children they had in her religion.

One potential source of conflict was Abdul's Islamic view of gender roles and of woman's place in the home. This was no difficulty for Martha, since she was raised in a family where her father ruled and her mother's life centered around the home. Martha had bought into that stereotyped role-casting. Hence, both Martha and Abdul were satisfied that they had enough compatibility in their religious beliefs so as to live comfortably with their differences.

The important element in both the story of Judith and Ambrose and that of Martha and Abdul is that they discussed the topic of their diverse religions and determined before the wedding date the impact these differences could have on their marriage. This kind of frank discussion is the most essential thing that couples who are planning interreligion marriages need to do.

Interdenominational Marriages

Interdenominational marriages are those that take place between two persons who belong to different denominations of the same religion. Within Christianity alone, there are more than two hundred denominations. Examples of interdenominational marriages are those between a Methodist and an Episcopalian, a Roman Catholic and a Presbyterian, a Baptist and a member of the Church of Christ, a Greek Orthodox Catholic and a Lutheran. Each of these denominations share the same basic religion, Christianity, but differ in their expression of it.

Since the Second Vatican Council there has been a marked change in attitude on the part of the Catholic Church and most Christian Churches. This change can be described as a shift from triumphalism, hostility and suspicion to understanding, appreciation, and cooperation. This improvement in relationship between the Christian Churches is one of the contributing factors to the rise in marriages between Catholics and Protestants in the past two and a half decades. This pattern of increase can be expected to continue. Here are some suggestions for Christians planning to enter an interdenominational marriage.

1. *Once your relationship begins to get serious, talk about your diverse religious backgrounds.* Probe the questions and issues that are likely to have an impact on your marriage. Avoid the attitude, "We can cross that bridge when we get to it. Our love will sustain us." One's religious heritage is often a much more significant element in a person's life than one thinks. The problems that diverse denominational affiliations can pose for a marital relationship are best confronted before the wedding day.

2. *A starting point for a couple's discussion is the common ground that the two Christian denominations share.* This serves as a constructive context for the later discussion of the differences that exist.

The most basic reality that Christian denominations share is Jesus Christ and his Gospel. Hence, a couple can begin by sharing with each other what they believe about Jesus, what significance he has for them, and what Gospel values they hold. There will indeed be differences in the way each person addresses these three issues. But these differences can be expressed within the same basic framework, namely, that Jesus and his Gospel are at the center of our life of Christian faith.

Teresa, a Catholic, and Bart, a Methodist, met while doing volunteer work at an interdenominational soup kitchen. One of the things that attracted them to each other was the deep commitment both of them had to living out in their own lives the love that Christ had for the poor and the downcast. While they worship in their separate churches, they read and pray the Scriptures together for fifteen minutes a day, and consistently work with each other on various projects for the needy. Teresa comments that her husband's Christian faith and commitment are much closer to her own than is the faith and value system of many Catholics she knows.

Even when the difference of a faith position of two Christians is more pronounced than in the case of Teresa and Bart, a couple can find common ground. Hugh had been raised as a Unitarian, and after college converted to the Society of Friends. While he continued to hold doubts about Jesus being the Son of God, he did see him as one specially anointed by God, and as the one who most perfectly revealed how humans ought to live. As a strict Baptist, Lucy believed strongly in the divinity of Jesus. At first Bart's vacillating about Jesus being God's Son disturbed her. She came, however, to see that, despite this difference in their belief, they both shared Jesus' vision and strove to follow his example.

3. *Measure precisely the denominational differences between the two of you.* There are two facets to this guideline. The first is to know something about the particular denomination to which your fiancé(e) is affiliated. There is a tendency, among some Catholics, for example, to put all Protestants into the same category, and to obscure the many differences that exist between

them. We have sometimes been asked, "What do you think of a Catholic marrying a Protestant?" The first answer to that is another question: "What kind of Protestant do you have in mind? Episcopalian, Lutheran, Quaker, Southern Baptist, Church of God?" Many of the Protestant churches are far apart from each other. Some, like the Episcopal Church, are much closer in structure and doctrine to the Catholic Church, while others, for example, the Churches of Christ, are extremely different. When it comes to preparing for marriage the comparison between "Catholic" and "Protestant" is not helpful. The comparison must be between Catholicism and the particular Protestant denomination to which one's fiancé(e) belongs.

The second facet to measuring the denominational differences between yourself and your fiancé(e) is to determine where s/he personally stands in relation to the official positions of her/his denomination. If s/he is Episcopalian, is s/he "high church" or "low church"? If s/he is Presbyterian, does s/he accept or reject Calvin's doctrine of predestination? It is a mistake to assume that each member of a denomination adheres to all of its official teachings and rulings.

4. *Discuss how you each feel about allowing the other to worship and to follow the practices of her/his denomination.* Does one of you expect the other to change? Are you agreed that each of you will go your separate ways in regard to religion? Or do you agree that both of you will participate at least occasionally in the other's worship and practices.

5. *Face the question of the religious formation of your children.* Explore how you both feel about your children being reared in the other's denomination. Can you come to a mutually satisfying agreement? If your fiancé(e)

belongs to a denomination that does not believe in infant baptism, how will that issue be resolved?

One couple we know decided that they would not rear the child in either religion. "We'll let the child decide when she is in high school or college." The difficulty with this approach is that the child is given no basis upon which to make a decision. Another couple exposed their children to both denominational churches, in order "to allow the children to choose between the two denominations, when they are ready." This approach is also problematic. The child is put in the difficult position of choosing between "mom's church" and "dad's church." For some children, at least, this might be tantamount to choosing between "mom" and "dad." A third couple we know agreed that half of the children would be raised in the father's denomination, and the other half in the mother's.

Many couples decide that it is best to raise the children in the denomination of one of the parents. Often this decision is made on the basis of how strongly one of the parents feels about her/his denomination. The difficulty, of course, arises if both feel very strongly that "all children in the marriage must be reared in my denomination." If this kind of conflict is detected during the courtship, it ought not be ignored until "after we are married." It ought to be resolved before the wedding. Inability to resolve this conflict could well be enough reason to call off the wedding.

Intradenominational Marriages

By "intradenominational" marriages we mean marriages between two people of the same denomination. We deliberately include this category under interfaith marriages for three reasons. First, sometimes more pronounced faith differences can exist between two people of the same denomination than exist between two people of different denominations. A "liberal" Catholic, for example, may have much more in common with an Episcopalian than with a conservative Catholic. Second, serious intradenominational differences can cause as much or more havoc to a marriage than do many interdenominational differences. Third, it is important to dispel the false assumption that there will be no religious conflicts if two persons of the same denomination marry each other. One Catholic father proclaimed recently, "My wife and I are so relieved that our daughter is marrying a Catholic, and not one of those Protestant people. At least, religion is one problem they won't have to face in their marriage." Perhaps, but perhaps not!

Karen and Gerald, both Catholics, had irreconcilable differences in regard to artificial contraception. He thought it was perfectly permissible. She clung strictly to the Roman Catholic prohibition.

Eileen and Henry, both members of the Missouri Synod of the Lutheran Church, could not work through the serious differences they had about interpreting the Bible. Henry took a literalist approach. Eileen thought such an approach was "ignorant and narrow."

While Kate and Arch were both devout Catholics, they were at an impasse in regard to the Mass. Kate came from a very traditionalist family that traveled twenty miles every Sunday to attend Latin Mass "in the old way." She considered the "new" Mass vulgar and "heretical." Arch had attended "guitar Masses" since his junior high school days. Neither could have anything to do with the other's form of worship.

Joan and Gabe had another kind of problem. Joan's Catholicism meant a great deal to her. Gabe, on the other hand, had been baptized, but had never received any formal religious education, and only went to church on Christmas and Easter. "Much as I love him," Joan commented, "I need someone with whom I can share my faith."

It is very important that each couple, though belonging to the same denomination, get in touch early with each other's faith life. They need to acquire a good understanding of where each of them is in regard to their denominational belief and practice. Are we able to share our denominational faith together? What are the areas of potential conflict? How can we address and resolve these?

Interracial Marriages

Marriages between Americans and Asians and between blacks and whites are becoming more prominent. In many parts of the country the American-Asian marriage has become more acceptable; the black-white marriage still raises eyebrows. Since the black-white marriage in the United States is socially the more problematic, we will limit our reflections to this type of interracial marriage.

The first thing we need to do in regard to this topic is to admit that deep inside each of us there lurks at least some racial prejudice. If we admit that, we can then address this prejudice and recognize it for what it is—irrational. It is this prejudice that explains why so many react irrationally to the very idea of a black-white marriage.

The next step is to look inside ourselves as parents or would-be parents. How would we feel if a daughter or son came home and announced that s/he was dating someone of another race, or, even further, that they were getting engaged? Why would we feel this way? Are we able to distinguish our reasonable concerns from our irrational, prejudicial reactions?

Reasonable concerns are those based on sound practical considerations. If they are reasonable, they can be discussed in a way that invites the other to enter into dialogue with us. "We love you and want your happiness. We will therefore support whatever decision you make. These, however, are our concerns." Among the reasonable concerns in this matter are whether the person has dated enough different people, and whether s/he has weighed sufficiently the consequences that an interracial marriage can have on the couple and on the children.

The expression of reasonable concerns is different from irrational reactions in several ways. First, it avoids derogatory remarks. It stays away from accusations: "You are just doing this to get back at us." If we are working out of reasonable concern, we do not put our daughter/son on guilt trips. "If you go through with this you will break our hearts." Nor do we try to manipulate the decision by undue pressure. "If you marry this person we won't attend the wedding, and you'll never cross our threshold again."

Responding reasonably to interracial marriage plans is much easier said than done. We do, however, prepare ourselves for such an eventuality, by growing in mature, authentic love for our children, and by growing in respect for their freedom and their right to make decisions.

On the other hand, a couple contemplating an interracial marriage need to ask themselves several questions. Are we handling this situation in ways that are as sensitive as possible to our families? Have we kept our motives free from any spirit of societal/parental rebellion or from any desire to shock? Have we gotten to know sufficiently each other's families, and are we comfortable in the different cultural situation? Are we strong enough as individuals and as a couple to withstand the pressures, prejudices and boorishness that will come our way because of present societal structures and attitudes? How will we provide an environment for our children that will be supportive enough for them to withstand the harsh realities of a prejudiced society?

None of these questions are aimed at discouraging an interracial marriage. These kinds of questions do serve the important purpose of helping a couple weigh the added burdens attached to an interracial marriage in a prejudiced society.

The Age Difference

Since it would be rather extraordinary to marry someone born on the same day, an age difference can be expected in almost all marriages. In the vast majority of these marriages the age differential is too minimal even to be a factor affecting the relationship. There is some point, however, at which the age difference is sufficiently notable as to become a factor to be considered in the relationship.

Where this point is to be located is difficult to determine. Is it seven years, twelve, twenty? In this range, we do not think there is any clear answer. Two factors come into play here. The first is: How old does a person actually look, act, and feel? If the woman is twenty-five and the man is forty, a telling determinant may be whether he has the appearance and energy of a thirty-three year old or a fifty year old. The second factor is how badly they want children of their own. If they want children and he is thirty-five while she is forty-five, the age difference is problematic.

Marriages where one spouse is thirty, forty, or fifty years older than the other represent clear-cut examples of dramatic age differences. To say this is not meant to discourage such marriages, but rather to alert people to weigh the special effects that such an age difference can have on the relationship.

We list here some of the issues that need to be considered by a couple when there is a notable age difference.

1. Is the couple prepared to withstand unkind and prejudicial judgments sometimes heard in regard to these kinds of marriages? More than once we have heard someone remark that the younger bride "is just looking for her father" or that the younger groom is "looking for his mother." Equally derogatory suggestions are sometimes made of the older spouse.

2. To what degree does their age difference reflect itself in their energy levels, their sex drives, their common interests? If there are age-related differences in these areas, can they be integrated into the marriage in a compatible way?

3. How will their difference in age affect their parenting? How will the couple work out any difficulties in this area?

4. Finally, the younger spouse ought to be prepared for the probability that s/he will be left a widow(er) at a relatively young age. Obviously, this can happen in any marriage. It is also possible that an older spouse may outlive a younger spouse. Nevertheless, the law of averages cannot be entirely ignored.

Summary

Where there are notable differences between the couple in the area of religion, race, or age, two extreme reactions are possible. On the one hand, there are voices to be heard that will say all such marriages are either doomed or highly risky. The other extreme is to pay little attention to these differences and to presume that they will work themselves out after the marriage.

Notable differences raise significant issues that need to be faced and discussed well before the wedding plans are finalized. These differences, however, must be evaluated, not in isolation, but in the context of the total relationship. Is the compatibility of the couple in other areas of the relationship strong enough to outweigh the difference and integrate it into the relationship. Or, given the makeup of the couple and the overall picture of the relationship, is the difference so pronounced as to be irreconcilable?

Reflection Exercises

For All Readers

What kinds of religious differences do you consider most problematic for a marriage?
What are your immediate reactions when you see a black-white couple?
How important do you think the comparative age factor is in a marriage?

For Married Couples

What have been the main similarities in your faith life and that of your spouse?
What have been the main differences?
How have these similarities and differences affected your ability to share your religious life with one another?
How have they affected the religious formation you have provided for your children?

For Engaged Couples

How do your religious beliefs, practices and ethical convictions compare with those of your fiancé(e)?
How do you hope to share your religious life after you are married?
Are there any religious differences that could cause problems (a) in your building marital intimacy; (b) in rearing your children? If so, how do you both intend to resolve these differences?

Chapter 10

Marriage and Christian Discipleship

When we began to write this book, a friend asked, "Is it going to be a religious book, or is it going to be practical?" We answered that for the most part it would be "explicitly practical, and implicitly religious." There ought to be no dichotomy between religion and the practical. Indeed, is religion at all authentic if it is not put into practice?

This book has focused on practical ways of living out the marriage commitment and achieving marital intimacy. However, while the book has explicitly centered on the practical, all of the concrete suggestions have flowed from Christian faith and a Christian value system. They are consistent with what it means to practice Christianity in the context of marriage and family life. This is what we mean when we say that all along the book has been "implicitly religious."

In this concluding chapter we wish to show how striving toward marital intimacy in the ways outlined in the preceding chapters is truly a living out of the Christian call to be followers of Jesus Christ. We write this chapter because so many Christians are not accustomed to associate what they do in their marriage as being at the very core of their life of faith and holiness. They tend to separate religion and look upon it as if it were something over and above their everyday married life. This kind of thinking is symptomatic of "the hour on Sunday is for God" syndrome. "You have the whole week for yourself," we have heard some preachers say. "Can't you give just one hour of it to God?" But if, as the ancient saying goes, "The glory of God is the human person fully alive," can we make that kind of separation? Aren't love of God, love of others and love of self three intrinsically linked sides of the same reality?

In this chapter, then, we want to show how fully living one's marriage and one's parenting is indeed at the heart of Christian holiness. Many people are much more prayerful and more holy than they realize. If they can become more consciously aware that what they are already doing at home pertains profoundly to the following of Christ, they can be helped to do it with more joyful dedication and enlightened inspiration, and with a feeling of greater self-worth.

In writing the chapter we have in mind people like Josie who some years ago complained: "I feel bad I'm not very religious. I hardly ever pray, I only go to church on Sunday, and I rarely participate in parish activities. I guess I'm too involved trying to be a good wife and mother." (Josie, at the time, had seven children at home ranging from the ages of five to seventeen. Her middle child was quite seriously handicapped.) Unfortunately, Josie had never quite gotten over her early Catholic training that associated holiness with celibacy. "I was always given the impression," Josie commented, "that marriage was for those who were not religious enough to dedicate themselves to God as priests and nuns."

The chapter is divided into three main parts, corresponding to three significant elements of Christian living: the sacramental dimension, sharing in Christ's mission, and some basic Christian virtues.

The Sacramental Dimension

Christianity is a sacramental religion, that is, it believes that God is present in the material visible reality of our human lives and touches and transforms us through that reality. It believes further that in an extraordinarily unique way God communicates to us through the human Jesus, God's Word enfleshed. As the Gospel of John puts it, "No one has ever seen God; it is the only Son, who is close to the Father's heart, who has made him known."

Another unique belief of Christianity is that Jesus who died is risen and continues to manifest his saving presence in and through the community of Christian believers. To the degree that Christians visibly manifest in their lives their faith, love and following of Christ, they are a sacrament, that is, a living sign of Christ's transforming presence and love.

In a very particular way, this is true in marriage. As the Pauline author of the Letter to the Ephesians makes clear in chapter five, the loving marriage between two Christian spouses, who are relating to each other as Christ wishes them to, is a sign of Christ's spousal relationship with the community of Christian believers. It is for this reason that Catholics call a marriage between two Christian believers a sacrament. While many Protestants prefer to reserve the term "sacrament" to baptism and Communion (also referred to as the Lord's supper or the Eucharist), they acknowledge the insight of Ephesians 5 that challenges Christian couples to manifest Christ's love in their marital relationship.

It is this insight that serves as a basis for a Christian spirituality of marriage. A truly Christian couple allow their daily lives to be influenced by their faith and love of Jesus, the Christ. They allow their experience of Jesus, especially in the sacraments of baptism, Eucharist, and reconciliation, to inspire and direct the way they regard and act toward each other. Let's make this more concrete by relating each of these last three mentioned sacraments to the daily living of marriage.

Baptism. When we are baptized we are called to be followers of Christ. If we take our baptism seriously, we spend the rest of our lives striving to enter into deeper friendship with Christ, and to grow in our ability to live the ideals of love and service that he proclaimed in the Gospel. For Christians who are called to marriage, married life becomes the primary context in which to live out their baptismal commitment. In faith the Christian couple experience Christ's love in and through the love they manifest for one another. Their intimate love for one another helps them perceive the depth and meaning of Christ's love. The qualities of Christ's love, as witnessed to in the Gospel, inspire the enrichment of their own love for one another.

Eucharist. In the commemoration of the Lord's supper, Christ gives us, in the bread and the wine, the gift of himself in friendship. "This is my body given for you." "This is the cup of my blood (my life) poured out for you." The experience of Communion enables the couple to go forth and to "do this in memory of (him)." The couple live the Eucharist by giving of their bodies, their lives, themselves to one another in the breaking of bread (and all the food and meals); in the sharing of the cup (the cup of blessings and joys, the cup of sorrows and tears); in being for one another (in the sexual expression of love and in all the moments—special and routine—of their life together).

Reconciliation. Love means having to say you are sorry. It also means challenging each other to be the best each can be. In the sacrament of reconciliation we say we are sorry. We also experience the forgiveness of Christ and receive the strength he gives us to strive toward higher ideals. The ritual expression of sorrow and forgiveness in the sacrament of reconciliation helps us to experience the same in our marriage. Apologizing, saying we are sorry to one another, and forgiving each other need to become a regular part of our married life. If this is done with sincerity, it leads to more serious striving toward greater sensitivity and love. Indeed, through this process of reconciliation with one another, we experience the forgiveness and healing grace of Christ.

Obviously, the sacramental experience of Christ in the marital relationship does not take place automatically. It requires two indispensable elements: faith in Christ and mutual love of the married partners. The deeper the couple's relationship with Christ and the more intimate their love for one another, the greater is the possibility for a couple to experience their marriage as a sacrament, a living sign of the love of Christ. Hence, everything that has been said in this book in regard to achieving intimacy with one's married partner pertains to a spirituality of the sacrament of marriage.

Sharing in Christ's Mission

The center of Jesus' mission was the proclamation and promotion of the kingdom or reign of God over the hearts and minds of humans. This is the mission that the risen Christ continues to carry on in and through his followers. Christians are called to allow God's goodness to reign in their lives and to influence the way they relate to one another. Basically this means that they strive to live their lives in unity and love, in truthfulness, justice and peace. It means that they serve rather than seek to be served, and that they grow in compassion with their fellow humans.

Obviously, the first place where a married couple are called to further the reign of God is in their own marriage. If they cannot promote the goodness of God there, where will they? On the other hand, if we genuinely experience God's goodness in our marriage, we are fortified to go forth and spread the good news beyond the four walls.

Again, this entire book on marital intimacy has been concerned about building into our marriage the very qualities associated with the kingdom or reign of God. Since everything we have written about marital intimacy pertains to fostering unity and love, no further elaboration is necessary here. We will reflect on how the other qualities of the kingdom just mentioned, namely, truthfulness, justice and peace, compassion and service, are an intrinsic part of a happy marriage.

Truthfulness is involved in all of the effort that a couple make to get in honest contact with themselves and their relationship. It is also promoted by every attempt to build good communication in the marriage, and to work through the complexities of various problems and conflicts.

Justice and Peace. The foundation for peace is justice. Sometimes people are reluctant to talk about practicing justice in marriage. "After all, marriage is about love. Justice is just the minimum." It is true that marriage must be a loving relationship, and hence cannot be reduced to a matter of respecting each other's rights. The difficulty, however, is that in the name of love, we can so easily overlook justice. Spouses can violate each other's right to privacy. They can denigrate one another's human dignity by name-calling and other forms of psychological and physical abuse. Spouses can take each other for granted. There can be a great deal of unfairness in the way household chores are divided (or not divided, as the case may be). Sexism can be deeply ingrained in the marriage. One could go on and on.

A large percentage of the quarrels, fights and sufferings in marriage is rooted in the injustices perpetrated. So, the first step to building peace in marriage is to practice basic human justice. We must respect each other as human beings who are equal in dignity, and equally deserving of regard for our God-given rights.

But the practice of justice in marriage goes even further than this. When persons pledge themselves as wife and husband, they give each other rights that no one else has in their regard: the right to marital love and intimacy, the right to a partnership of life and love. Hence, spouses assume in justice obligations and responsibilities to one another to create a mutually satisfying and happy married life.

Infidelity to one's marital vows goes far beyond the commission of adultery. It includes all the ways we can renege on our commitment to create an intimate marriage. Marital infidelity, in all of its meanings, does not just violate the covenant of love. It is also a violation of justice. It is a refusal to give to one's spouse what is her/his due.

We cannot then distinguish between justice and love in marriage according to some longitudinal line: to be just I must go this far; beyond this point is love. No. Rather, justice and love are two distinguishable but inseparable dimensions of the total relationship. Injustice to one's spouse is a violation of love. Failure to love one's spouse is a violation of justice. In other words, there is a justice dimension to our marital love. Once we have pronounced our marriage vows we owe each other our spousal love.

The best way to secure peace in a marriage is to practice justice (and, hence, love). When justice is violated in a marriage we need to have the courage to confront it. "I feel that you are not doing your fair share of the household tasks." "I feel belittled by the snide remarks you make to me in front of your friends." "I feel you need to give me more space."

If we do not confront our spouse with the injustices of which s/he is guilty, there will be no real peace, but merely a superficial calmness. Such a calmness can conceal only for a while the growing anger underneath. True peace must be made. And it is made by confronting injustice, though such confrontation often causes disturbance before it creates peace.

Compassion and Service. The preceding chapters have indicated many of the ways in which a couple who are striving for marital intimacy need to grow in compassion and empathy and give of themselves in service to one another. Since we are emotional and not just thinking human beings, oneness with our spouse demands that we be able to "enter" into each other and be in touch with one another's feelings.

Such compassion and empathy make us sensitive to the deeper spiritual and psychological needs of one another. This leads us to respond to each other and serve not only our spouse's physical needs, but even more importantly her/his spiritual and emotional longings.

If couples are truly working at creating an intimate marriage, they are promoting the Christ-like qualities of unity and love, of truthfulness, justice and peace, and of compassion and service. They are, in other words, already making present in their marriage the kingdom (the reign) of God. Since families are an integral part of the Church and of human society, to allow God to reign in our marriages and our family life is to advance God's kingdom in the whole world.

Christian Virtues

There are many virtues traditionally associated with the following of Christ. A number of these have already been considered in our discussion of the sacramental dimension of marriage, and the Christian couple's responsibility to advance the kingdom (reign) of God. In concluding our treatment of marriage and Christian discipleship we want to reflect on several other virtues that are required for authentic marital intimacy.

Trusting Faith. Perhaps one of the profoundest acts of faith a couple make is when they walk to the altar and exchange their marriage vows. Even though they love each other, and have good reasons to be convinced of their compatibility, they face an uncertain future. So, in a sense, their marital commitment involves a leap into the dark. They exchange their promises because they believe in one another's love, integrity and fidelity, despite the fact that the presence of these qualities cannot be proven beyond a shadow of a doubt.

Making the marriage commitment involves faith in oneself. "I believe I am a good, stable person, capable of being a loving and faithful companion who can bring happiness to my spouse."

Fidelity to the marital commitment also requires belief in the value of marriage itself. Why be married? Why be committed to only one person in sexual love? Why build an intimate and lasting bond until death? These are the kinds of questions that face all of us. To respond to these questions in a positive way, one needs to believe that there is more to life than mere physical gratification, and that there is a spiritual value to integrating sexuality with love and commitment. Indeed, saying "I do" and living it require belief that the psalmist is right in claiming that "love is built to last forever" (Ps 89:2).

Finally, for the Christian believer commitment to marriage involves faith in God and in Christ. The Lord becomes the source of strength who graces our lives, inspires our love, and shines as the ultimate beacon of hope that life has meaning and purpose, and that all authentic intimacy in this life leads to the fulfillment of intimacy in the next.

Prayerfulness. Basically, prayer is the human response to God who is already communicating to humans. The center of one's prayer life is an awareness of God's presence and love, and the response one makes to this presence in thought, word, and action.

Many times during the day a person can momentarily reflect on this presence of God and of Christ. This can be done while working at a desk, cooking, driving the car, doing the laundry, cutting the grass, and in the midst of all the other endless tasks that engage us in the routine of our lives.

Sometimes this reflection may be a brief thought without words. At other times it may be a spontaneous prayer of praise, of thanks, of petition. Frequently, when we feel almost overwhelmed by a cluttered room that needs straightening, or a paper-filled desk that has to be sorted through, or a messy kitchen that needs to be cleaned, a rhythmic reciting of a familiar prayer like the "Our Father" helps calm us as we tackle the unwieldy disorder.

Perhaps a person is able to put several minutes aside to pray and reflect quietly, uninhibited by other distractions. Once in a while a couple may want to spend some of their time praying together.

For couples who take seriously the fact that their marriage is a sacrament, a living sign of Christ's love, the entire married life becomes a prayer. Even when not consciously adverting to it, they are aware in a general way of Christ's presence and love in their intimacy with one another. Accordingly, all of their responses in love to one another can become a response to the love of God and of Christ.

Humility. In the past there was a common misunderstanding about this virtue. Humility was often confused with self-debasement and thinking poorly of oneself. In some spiritual formation programs, a deliberate effort was made to humiliate people, under the false assumption that humiliation would bring about humility.

Actually, to be humble is to make an honest and accurate assessment of oneself. Humility avoids the extremes of having too high or too low an opinion of oneself. The humble person does not think s/he is better or worse than s/he really is.

In a number of places in this book we have stressed the need for a good self-image if one is to be able to relate intimately with one's partner. Humility is possessing a true self-image. It is esteeming oneself according to one's real worth.

Chastity. Too often chastity has been identified with celibacy and sexual abstinence. However, chastity is a virtue incumbent on every Christian. It is a lifelong process whereby a person integrates her/his sexuality in terms of becoming a fully alive and loving human being. In marriage the essence of chastity is to direct one's sexual energies and drives toward the building of a permanent, exclusive, intimate and life-giving relationship with one's spouse. All of the discussion and suggestions presented in the chapter on sexuality feed into an understanding of what Christian chastity is all about.

Concern for the Poor and the Underprivileged. There are two levels at which this virtue has to be practiced: the attitudinal and the practical. On the attitudinal level a married couple need to ask themselves what their thoughts and feelings are when they see, hear, and read about the jobless, the poverty-stricken, and the disadvantaged. Do we blame the poor? "It's their own fault." "They are just lazy." "There are enough jobs for everyone. They just don't want to bother looking for them." Do we harbor such prejudices? Or, rather, do we allow the established sociological and economic facts to correct these common misunderstandings?

Also, on the attitudinal level, how do we emotionally react when we drive through a poor neighborhood? Are our predominant feelings those of compassion and a desire to do something to alleviate deprivation? Or do we mostly experience snobbish feelings of disdain for the poor and of haughtiness because of our own perceived "position of superiority"?

When we are standing in line at the checkout counter of the supermarket and see "the black woman with food stamps and a steak in her basket" (which we hear so much about from middle class whites), what are our feelings? Are we incensed? Are we jealous? Or are we glad that at least occasionally her family has an opportunity to eat like the rest of us? If we are dismayed "because this is our hard-earned money paid in taxes," are we proportionately disturbed by the luxurious state dinners at the White House, the staggering wastes at the Defense Department, and the enormous tax breaks for large corporations and millionaires? After all, that, too, is "our hard-earned money."

On the practical level, couples need to open their hearts and their purses to the poor and needy. They can share some of their time and energy alleviating the physical, emotional and educational needs of the disadvantaged. In doing so, they believe that "insofar as you did this to one of the least of these brothers of mine, you did it to me" (Mt 25:40).

Summary

One of the most intimate scenes portrayed in the Gospel is the Last Supper. Jesus is gathered with his closest companions for his last meal before his death. Luke has Jesus saying, "I have longed to eat this passover with you before I suffer" (Lk 22:15).

John introduces the Last Supper scene by commenting that Jesus "had always loved those who were his in the world, but now he showed how perfect his love was" (Jn 13:1). During the meal he washed his disciples' feet and gave them bread and wine as a sign of the gift of his own life. He called them "friends" and stressed the need for love. He promised not to leave them orphans, and asked that their hearts not be troubled. He wished for them peace and joy, and wanted them to be united to him as branches are to a vine. At the end of the supper, Jesus summed up his desire for his disciples in this prayer, "May they all be one. Father, may they be one in us, as you are in me and I am in you" (Jn 17:21).

Marriage for Christians is a sacrament, a sign of Christ's love for us, the kind of love he demonstrated at the Last Supper. We experience the intimacy of Christ's love in the intimate relationship we have with our spouse. The closeness and love, the intimate caring and concern, the peace and the joy found in a happy marriage reveal what Christ desires for all of us, and what he has prepared for us in the kingdom of God. For, indeed, this kingdom is, as Jesus made clear, like a wedding feast.

Reflection Exercises

For All Readers

How can marriage for two baptized persons be a form of Christian discipleship?
Explain whether or not it is really relevant to everyday life to speak of the sacramental dimension of marriage.
Besides the virtues discussed in this chapter, what other virtues are important for an intimate, happy marriage?

For Married Couples

In what ways have you experienced your marriage as a sacrament, a sign of Christ's love?
What practical suggestions do you have for making your marriage more sacramental?
Which of the virtues discussed in the last section of the

chapter are the ones most strongly present in your marriage?
Which are the ones that could be strengthened? How?

For Engaged Couples

In light of your relationship thus far, what hopes do you have for living a truly Christian marriage?
In what ways do you think this might be difficult to accomplish?
What practical suggestions do you have for allowing Christ's love to be manifested more fully in your relationship?